100 *Deadly* Opening Traps in Chess

And How Not to Get Caught!
From Beginner to Experienced Expert

Bob Ischiffer

Copyright © Bob Ischiffer, 2024. All rights reserved.
ISBN: 9798312840094

Symbols & Abbreviations

□ White traps Black

■ Black traps White

Trap leading to checkmate

♕ White loses a queen

♛ Black loses a queen

♖ White loses a rook

♜ Black loses a rook

♗ White loses a bishop

♝ Black loses a bishop

♘ White loses a knight

♞ Black loses a knight

♙ White loses a pawn

♟ Black loses a pawn

W- White loses the exchange

B- Black loses the exchange

± White has the advantage

∓ Black has the advantage

+ - Decisive advantage for White

- + Decisive advantage for Black

The statistical data is sourced from the Lichess database.

Table of content

Introduction: Humans on the Chessboard..................1

The Italian Game..................................3

   1. A classic to start: Legal's Mate....................3

   2. The Belloni Trap...................................4

   3. Lateral Attack.....................................5

   4. On the Giuoco Piano................................6

   5. The Rosentreter Gambit.............................7

   6. An Explosive Gambit................................8

   7. Don't Play Passively!..............................9

   8. The Blackburne Trap...............................10

   9. A Blackburne Variation............................11

   10. The Queen in the Bag............................12

   11. Black Counterattacks.............................13

   12. Two Raging Knights..............................14

   13. A Little-Known Variation........................15

The Ruy Lopez...................................16

   14. Breyer's Sardine Trap...........................16

   15. Gonzalez Zamora's Trap..........................17

   16. The Noah's Ark Trap.............................18

   17. The Fishing Pole Trap...........................19

   18. The Mortimer Trap...............................20

The Sicilian Defense 21

19. The Poisoned Pawn in the Najdorf 21

20. A False Gift 22

21. The Non-Capture on d4 23

22. The Tempting Pawn 24

23. A Troublesome Knight 25

24. A Hole in the Defense 26

25. A Surprising Gambit 27

26. A French Variation 28

27. A Trap Against the Grand Prix Attack 29

28. The Siberian Trap 30

29. Another Trap in the Smith-Morra Gambit 31

The French Defense 32

30. Chernev's Greek Gift 32

31. Queen in Check 33

32. Fatal Fork 34

33. Two's Company 35

34. Morphy's Trap 36

35. The Tables Turned 37

The Caro-Kann Defense 38

36. The Anand-Carlsen Theme 38

37. Mate in 6 Moves! 39

38. A Quality Trap..40

39. Bishops on the File...41

The Scotch Game..42

40. A Stranded Bishop..42

41. The Nd2 Trap...43

42. Quick Mate...44

43. A Overpowering Pawn......................................45

The Göring Gambit...46

44. The Gunner Bishop..46

The Three Knights Game..47

45. Winning Combo...47

The Russian Defense or Petrov..................................48

46. A Bad Pin..48

47. The Stafford Gambit Trap..................................49

The Philidor Defense..50

48. The Famous f7 Square.......................................50

49. Don't Play Passively!..51

The Ponziani Opening..52

50. The Flagship Trap...52

The Vienna Game...53

51. A Beautiful Mate..53

52. The Queen Steps Out...54

The Bishop's Opening 55
- 53. Fatal Assault 55
- 54. Queen Exchange 56

The Center Game 57
- 55. Goodbye, Madam! 57

The Danish Gambit 58
- 56. Queen in the Center 58
- 57. The Danish Bird Trap 59

The King's Gambit 60
- 58. Queen or Mate? 60
- 59. Quick Mate 61
- 60. A (Too) Greedy Queen 62

The Scandinavian Defense 63
- 61. The Tennison Trap 63
- 62. Queen vs Queen 64
- 63. Valencian Variation 65
- 64. Imperfect Pin 66
- 65. The Icelandic Gambit 67

The Pirc/Modern Defense 68
- 66. Fatal Retreat 68
- 67. The Suffocated Queen 69

Alekhine Defense 70

68. A Strange King Move..70

69. The King is Exposed...71

70. The O'Sullivan Gambit..72

Nimzowitsch Defense...73

71. Knight Collapse..73

Gunderam Defense..74

72. The Fragile Knight..74

1. e4 – Other Openings..75

73. Busch-Gass Gambit..75

74. The Premature Attack..76

The Queen's Gambit..77

75. The Rubinstein Trap...77

76. A White Classic...78

77. A Black Classic..79

78. Counterattack in the Center.......................................80

The Slav Defense...81

79. A False Pin..81

The Nimzo-Indian Defense...82

80. One Step Too Far..82

The King's Indian Defense..83

81. The Ng4 Trap in the Saemisch....................................83

The Queen's Indian Defense...84

    82. A Beautiful Diagonal..84

The Benoni Defense..85
    83. A Mirrored Trap..85

Other Indian Defenses...86
    84. The Alekhine-Marshall Trap...........................86

The London System..87
    85. The Trapped Queen...87
    86. The Poor Bishop...88

The Jobava Attack..89
    87. Eyes on c7!...89

The Stonewall Attack..90
    88. Pawn Wave..90

The Torre Attack..91
    89. Queen on the Horizontal...............................91

The Albin Counter-Gambit...92
    90. Lasker's Trap..92

The Budapest Gambit..93
    91. The Fajarowicz Trap.......................................93

The Blackmar-Diemer Gambit..................................94
    92. The Halosar Trap..94

The Dutch Defense..95
    93. The X Factor..95

- 94. A Miniature...96
- The Englund Gambit..97
  - 95. The Englund Gambit Trap...................................97
  - 96. A Queen or Nothing...98
  - 97. Again, a Queen or Nothing.................................99
- The English Opening..100
  - 98. English Trap for Beginners...............................100
  - 99. The Untouchable Queen..................................101
- Other Openings...102
  - 100. A Strange Checkmate....................................102
- Acknowledgments...103
- Share Your Thoughts...104

Introduction: Humans on the Chessboard

« Chess is 99 percent tactics. » - Richard Teichmann

The theory of openings and the development of chess engines have evolved so much that today we can clearly distinguish good moves from bad ones, particularly in the opening. As a result, no one should fall for even the smallest trap anymore. Except that...

We are not machines, and we make mistakes—and that's a good thing! It's part of what makes this game beautiful and gives it its fun, human side. Who hasn't felt the joy of setting up a trap in advance? It doesn't happen in every game, of course, but when it does, what a satisfaction it is!

On the other hand, who hasn't experienced the frustration of falling into a trap set by our opponent, just when we thought we had a solid position—or even a winning one? This often happens, actually. A trap is sometimes a desperate weapon to escape a bad situation. A moment of inattention from the stronger player, and the entire game can be turned upside down, sometimes even ending in a smart checkmate.

This book presents 100 opening traps. Some are well-known, others less so. These traps are organized by opening and apply to both White and Black. The major openings include more traps since they feature a greater number of variations. The Italian Game, being the most commonly played at the amateur level (though not only there!), is particularly well-represented. A small symbol indicates the damage inflicted on players who fall for these traps.

Learn the traps related to the openings you play so that you can both use them effectively and avoid falling into them. You can try out some traps in casual games, for example by playing blitz online. Avoid those that belong to dubious openings when playing in tournaments, as if they fail, you may find yourself in trouble—especially if your opponent has plenty of time to think.

I hope you enjoy studying these traps as much as I enjoyed presenting them to you, and that you'll soon have the pleasure of springing a few of them on your opponents! Have fun and good luck to everyone!

The Italian Game

The Italian Game begins with the moves 1. e4 e5 2. Nf3 Nc6 3. Bc4

1. A classic to start: Legal's Mate
□ #

1. e4 e5 2. Nf3 Nc6 3. Bc4 d6?! 4. Nc3 Bg4 5. h3 Bh5?

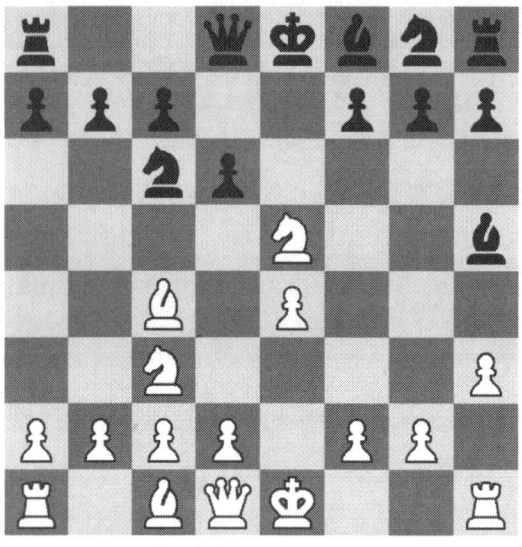

6. Nxe5!

Bxd1?? 7. Bxf7+ Ke7 8. Nd5#

How to avoid the trap : 5... Bxf3 6. Qxf3 Nf6 and Black can continue their development.

It should be noted that Legal's Mate can also occur through the Philidor Defense: 1. e4 e5 2. Nf3 d6 3. Bc4 Bg4 4. Nc3 g6 5. Nxe5 Bxd1 6. Bxf7+ Ke7 7. Nd5#. The mistake here is 4... g6, intending to fianchetto the f8 bishop. Instead, Black should play 4... Nc6, and after 5. h3, exchange on f3 as in the Italian Game.

2. The Belloni Trap

1. e4 e5 2. Nf3 Nc6 3. Bc4 Bc5 4. c3 d6 5. d4 exd4 6. cxd4 Bb4+

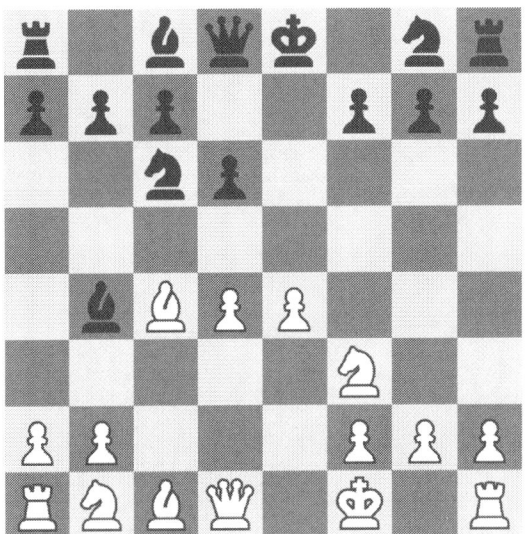

7. Kf1

This move might seem counterintuitive because it displaces the white king, prevents castling, and traps the h1 rook. However, Black has very few good options here. White will exploit the pin on the Nc6 to threaten the Bb4. For example:

- 7... Nf6 8. d5 Ne5 9. Nxe5 dxe5 10. Qa4+ Bd7 11. Qxb4
- 7... Bg4 8. Qb3 Bxf3 9. gxf3 Qf6 10. Bb5 Ne7 11. Qxb4

How to avoid the trap :

Black gains nothing by checking the white king with Bb4+. Playing 6... Bb6 is much safer and allows Black to continue their development.

3. Lateral Attack

1. e4 e5 2. Nf3 Nc6 3. Bc4 Bc5 4. c3 Nf6 5. d3 d5? 6. exd5 Nxd5 7. Qb3! (attacking both Nd5 and f7) Be6 (7... Nce7 8. Qb5+) 8. Qxb7 Na5

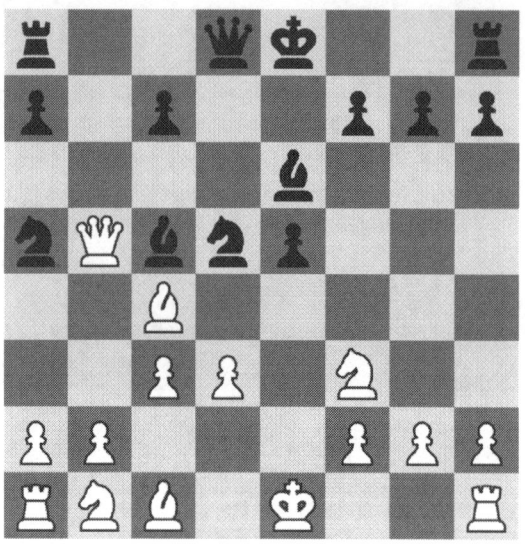

9. Qb5+

c6

10. Qxc5

How to avoid the trap

The direct central counterattack 5... d5? is not good. Black should instead play the modest 5... d6, castle, and continue developing in what remains an equal position for now.

4. On the Giuoco Piano
□ #

1. e4 e5 2. Nf3 Nc6 3. Bc4 Bc5 4. c3 Nf6 5. d4 exd4 6. cxd4 Bb4+ 7. Nc3 Nxe4 8. O-O Nxc3 9. bxc3 Be7

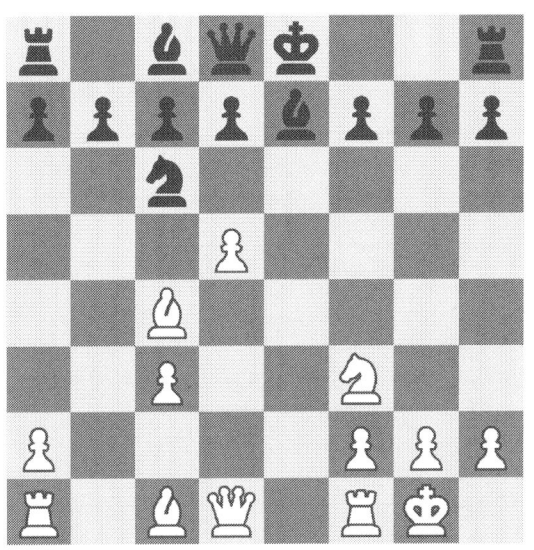

10. d5

Na5 11. d6 Bxd6 (11... Nxc4 12. dxe7 Qxe7 13. Re1 traps the queen) 12. Re1+ Be7 13. Bg5 f6 14. Bxf6 gxf6 15. Ne5 fxe5 16. Qh5+ Kf8 17. Qf7#

Note that after 15... h5 16. Qd5 Rf8 17. Be2! White mates in two moves no matter how Black defends.

How to avoid the trap

8... Bxc3 9. d5 Bf6 is preferable, although 8... Nxc3 is still playable. However, after 9. bxc3, the only move for Black is the central counterstrike 9... d5, or they will face major problems. For example: 9... Bxc3? 10. Ba3! (stopping Black from castling) d5 (too late!) 11. Bb5 Bxa1 12. Re1+ Be6 13. Qc2! Qd7 14. Ne5 Qc8 15. Bxc6+ bxc6 16. Qxc6+, and Black's position collapses with mate to follow.

5. The Rosentreter Gambit
□ ±

1. e4 e5 2. Nf3 Nc6 3. Bc4 Bc5 4. d4 exd4 5. c3 dxc3? (5... Nf6 6. e5 d5!)

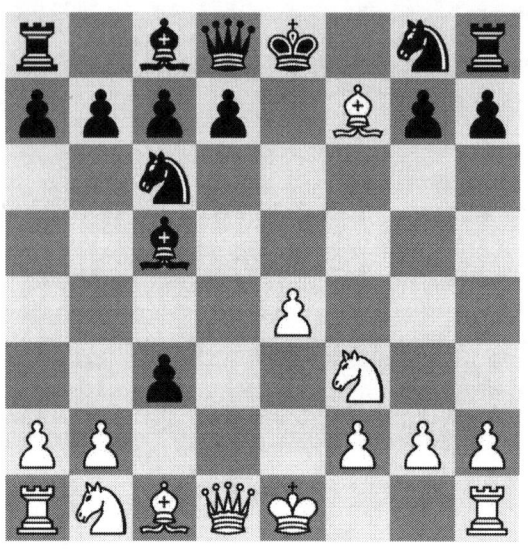

6. Bxf7+

Kxf7

7. Qd5+ Ke8 8. Qh5+ g6

9. Qxc5

How to avoid the trap

4... Nxd4 is possible, but be careful with 5. Be3 Nxf3+? (Qf6!) 6. Qxf3, as the black bishop is lost due to the threat of mate on f7. The best move is 4... Bxd4 5. Nxd4 Nxd4, and after, for example, 6. Be3 Nc6 7. Qh5 Qe7 8. Nc3 Nf6, the position is equal.

6. An Explosive Gambit
□ + -

1. e4 e5 2. Nf3 Nc6 3. Bc4 Nf6 4. d4 exd4 5. O-O Nxe4 6. Nc3?! dxc3 7. Bxf7+ Kxf7 8. Qd5+ Ke8 9. Re1 Be7 10. Rxe4 d6 11. Bg5 Rf8 12. Rae1 Rf7? (cxb2!)

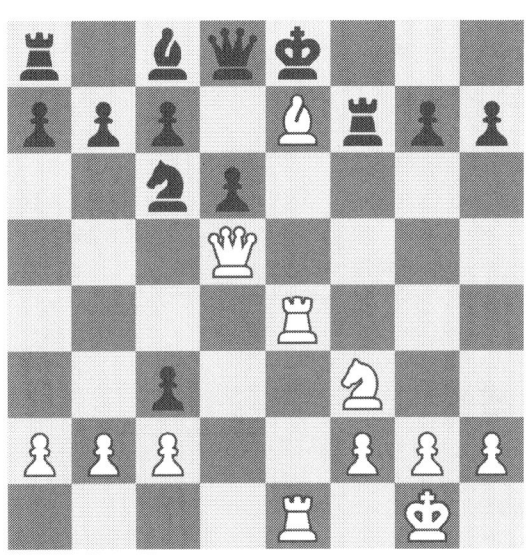

13. Bxe7

Nxe7 14. Ng5 Rf5 15. Qg8+ Kd7 16. Qxg7 Re5 17. Rxe5 dxe5 18. Rd1+ and the queen is lost (18... Ke8 19. Qf7#)

How to avoid the trap

This gambit is not sound for White but it is dangerous. Countless venomous variations exist, which the format of this book does not allow us to explore in detail. The best option for Black is to avoid getting entangled in complications and castle quickly: 6... Nxc3 7. bxc3 Be7 8. cxd4 d5 9. Bb5 O-O. True, Black has only a pawn rather than a piece, but White has no positional advantage.

7. Don't Play Passively!

□ ♕/♙ + -

1. e4 e5 2. Nf3 Nc6 3. Bc4 h6?! 4. d4 d6 (4... exd4 5. Nxd4 Nxd4 6. Qxd4 leaves Black with little chance) 5. dxe5 Nxe5 6. Nxe5 dxe5

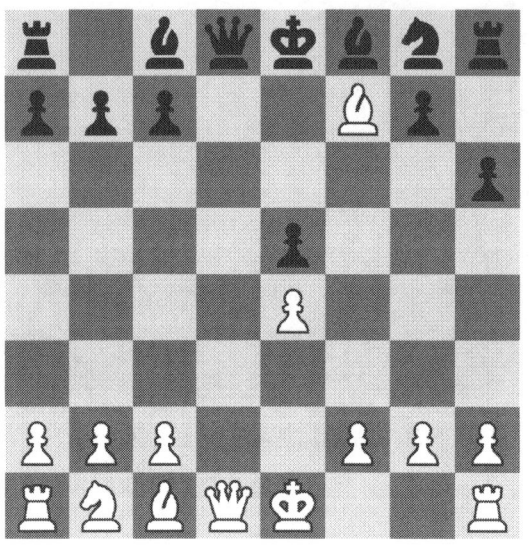

7. Bxf7+

Ke7 (7... Kxf7 8. Qxd8) 8. Qf3

How to avoid the trap

The move 3... h6 is often played at the amateur level (+2.4M in the database!). Black wants to play Nf6 without fearing Ng5 and the attack on f7. But this move is too passive and allows White to attack the center. The classical moves Bc5 and Nf6 are the best options. Study them!

8. The Blackburne Trap
■ #

1. e4 e5 2. Nf3 Nc6 3. Bc4 Nd4?! 4. Nxe5?!

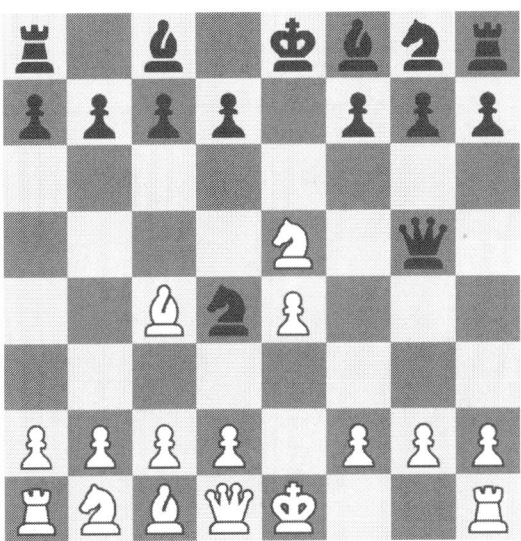

4... Qg5!

5. Nxf7 Qxg2 6. Rf1 Qxe4+ 7. Be2 Nf3#

How to avoid the trap

White must not be too greedy. After 3... Nd4 4. Nxd4 exd4 5. d3, White has the advantage thanks to a lead in development and a better pawn structure.

9. A Blackburne Variation
■ #

1. e4 e5 2. Nf3 Nc6 3. Bc4 Nf6 4. Ng5 d5 5. exd5 Nd4 6. d6 Qxd6! 7. Nxf7

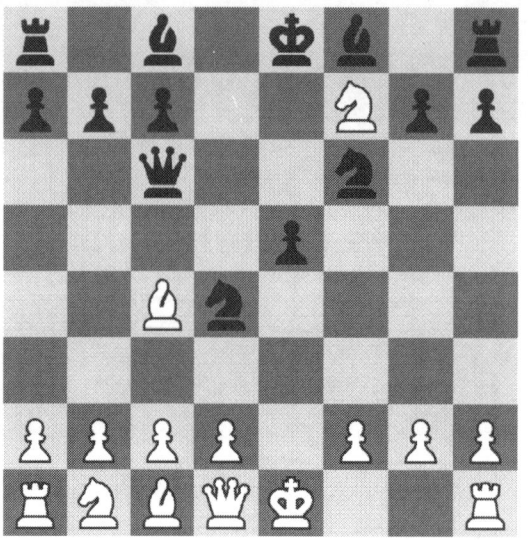

7... Qc6

8. Nxh8 Qxg2 9. Rf1 Qe4+ 10. Be2 Nf3#

How to avoid the trap

As in the previous trap, the f7 pawn cannot be captured due to the double attack on Bc4 and the g2 pawn. White must play 6. c3 to drive away the Nd4, and after 6... Nf5 7. Qe2, White is better.

10. The Queen in the Bag
■ #

1.e4 e5 2.Nf3 Nc6 3.Bc4 Bc5 4.d3 Nf6 5.0–0 d6 6.Bg5 h6 7.Bh4 g5 8.Bg3 h5 9.Nxg5 h4 10.Nxf7

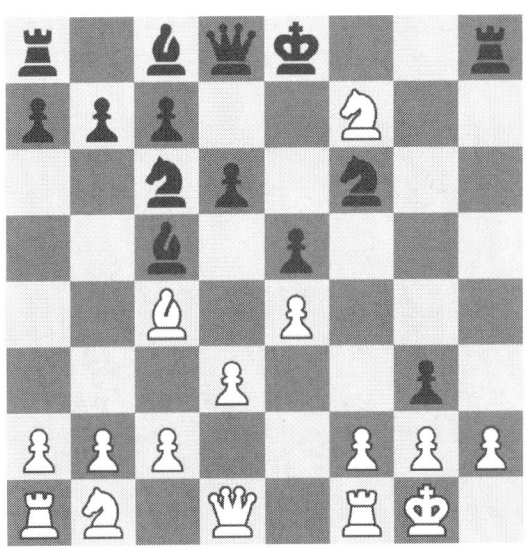

10... hxg3

(offers the queen)

11.Nxd8 Bg4 12.Qd2 Nd4 13.h3 Ne2+ 14.Kh1 Rxh3+ 15.gxh3 Bf3#

If 13. Nc3 to prevent Ne2+, then follows 13... Nf3+! 14. gxf3 Bxf3 and the mate by Rh1 is unstoppable.

How to avoid the trap

It is safer for White not to capture the g5 pawn and instead play 9. h4, and now for example:
- 9... Bg4 10. c3! Prepares b4 and allows the white queen to reach c3
- 9... g4 10. Ng5 gives White good chances

11. Black Counterattacks
■ #

1. e4 e5 2. Nf3 Nc6 3. Bc4 Bc5 4. d3 f5 5. Ng5 f4 6. Nf7 Qh4 7. O-O Nf6 8. Nxh8

8... Ng4

9. h3 Nxf2 10. Rxf2 Qxf2+ 11. Kh1 f3 12. gxf3 d5 13. Bxd5 Bxh3 and mate is unstoppable.

How to avoid the trap

Capturing the rook on a8 is the fatal mistake. Instead, White should play 8. Nd2 followed by Nf3 to protect h2 and drive away the queen, but the simplest solution is to play 5. Nc3 Nf6 6. O-O to speed up development.

12. Two Raging Knights
■ ♖ ♙

1. e4 e5 2. Nf3 Nc6 3. Bc4 Nf6 4. Ng5 Nxe4 5. Nxf7 Qh4 6. O-O

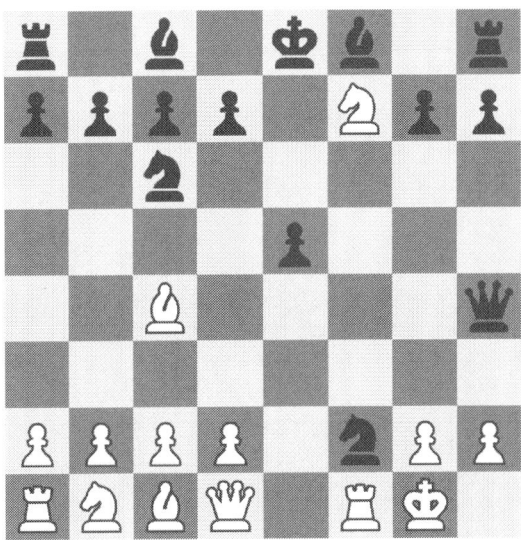

6... Nxf2

7. Rxf2 Bc5 8. Qf3 Rf8 9. g3 Bxf2+ 10. Qxf2 Qxc4 11. d3 Qxf7 12. Qxf7+ Rxf7

How to avoid the trap

This rare variation is full of traps. 5. Nxe4 doesn't work because of 5... d5. The correct move is 5. Bxf7+ Ke7, but caution is needed. The most played moves — 6. Nxe4 Kxf7 7. Qf3+ Ke8 8. d3 d5 9. Ng5 Qf6 10. Qxd5 Nd4 11. Qc4 b5 12. Qc3 Bb4 — lose the white queen! The move 6. d4! h6 7. Nxe4 Kxf7 8. d5! Nd4 9. c3 gives White the advantage due to Black's exposed king.

13. A Little-Known Variation
■ ♛

1. e4 e5 2. Nf3 Nc6 3. Bc4 f5 The Rousseau Gambit 4. exf5 e4 5. Qe2 Qe7 6. Ng1 Nf6 7. d3

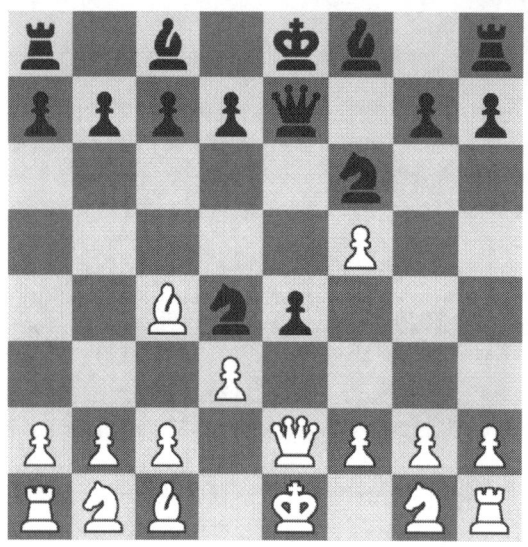

7... Nd4

8. Qd2 Nxc2+ 9. Qxc2 exd3+

How to avoid the trap

After 5. Nd4, the white knight cannot be captured because 5... Nxd4 6. Qh5+ g6 7. fxg6 Qf6 8. g7+ Kd8 9. gxh8=Q Qxh8 10. Bxg8 Qxg8 11. O-O leaves Black without enough time to take the Ra1: 11... Nxc2 12. Nc3 Nxa1 13. Nd5, and Black's king is too exposed.
The best response is to counterattack with 4. d4! fxe4 5. Nxe5 d5 6. Bb5, giving White good play.

The Ruy Lopez

The Ruy Lopez begins with the moves 1. e4 e5 2. Nf3 Nc6 3. Bb5

14. Breyer's Sardine Trap
□ ♛

1. e4 e5 2. Nf3 Nc6 3. Bb5 a6 4. Ba4 Nf6 5. O-O Be7 6. Re1 b5 7. Bb3 d6 8. c3 O-O 9. h3 Nb8 10. d4 Nbd7 11. Nbd2 Re8?

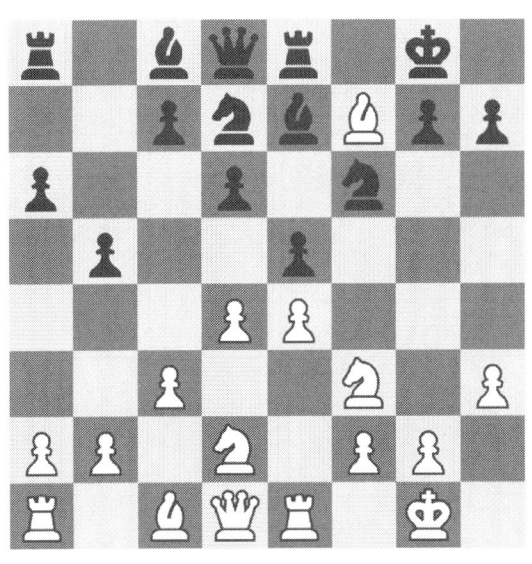

12. Bxf7+!

Kxf7 13. Ng5+ Kg8 14. Ne6

How to avoid the trap

Black must not allow their queen to get trapped. 11... Bb7, which continues development, keeps options open for both sides.

15. Gonzalez Zamora's Trap
□ #

1. e4 e5 2. Nf3 Nc6 3. Bb5 a6 4. Ba4 Nf6 5. O-O Be7 6. Re1 b5 7. Bb3 d6 8. c3 O-O 9. h3 Bb7 10. d4 Re8 11. dxe5 dxe5

12. Bxf7+

Kxf7 13. Qb3+ Kg6 14. Nh4+ Kh5 15. Qf7+ g6 16. Nf5 Rh8 17. Qxf6 Bxf6 18. g4#

How to avoid the trap

The first mistake is 11... dxe5. It is better for Black to recapture with the knight to force the exchange of the Nf3 and prevent any sacrifice of the bishop on b3 targeting f7. The second, more serious mistake is the black king fleeing to g6, which opens the way to mate. Here, Black must return the piece with 13... Nd5. Even though White remains better, the game is not yet lost.

16. The Noah's Ark Trap

1. e4 e5 2. Nf3 Nc6 3. Bb5 a6 4. Ba4 d6 5. d4 b5 6. Bb3 Nxd4 7. Nxd4 exd4

8. Qxd4??

8... c5!

9. Qd5 Be6 10. Qc6+ Bd7 11. Qd5 c4 and the bishop on b3 is lost.

How to avoid the trap

8. c3 dxc3 9. Nxc3, and despite being a pawn down, the position is equal due to White's lead in development.

17. The Fishing Pole Trap
■ #

1. e4 e5 2. Nf3 Nc6 3. Bb5 Nf6 4. O-O Ng4 5. h3

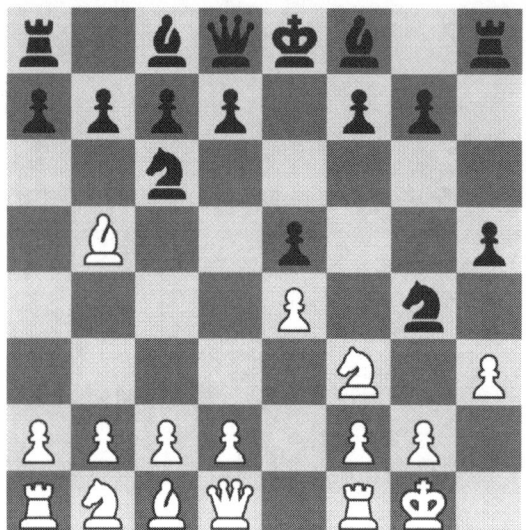

5... h5

6. hxg4 hxg4 7. Ne1 Qh4
8. f3 g3 9. d4 Qh2#

How to avoid the trap

After 5... h5, White responds with 6. c3! followed by d4, seizing the center and the initiative.

18. The Mortimer Trap

■ ♗ ou ♘

1. e4 e5 2. Nf3 Nc6 3. Bb5 Nf6 4. d3 Ne7 5. Nxe5?

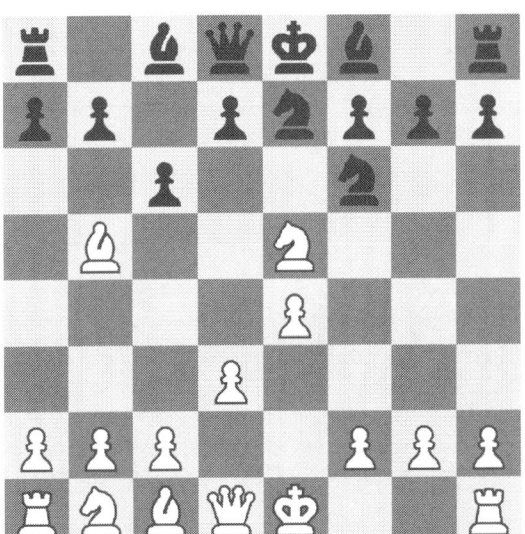

5... c6!

If the Bb5 moves, then 6... Qa5+ follows, losing the Ne5. White can try 6. Nc4, which covers a5 and threatens mate on d6, but after 6... Ng6 7. e5 Nd5 8. Qf3 cxb5, they will play a piece down. If 6. Nxf7 Kxf7 7. Bc4+ d5, Black's king will have time to find safety, and White has no compensation for the knight.

How to avoid the trap

With the e5 pawn untouchable, White must castle and develop normally.

The Sicilian Defense

The Sicilian Defense begins with the moves 1. e4 c5

19. The Poisoned Pawn in the Najdorf
□ ♛

1. e4 c5 2. Nf3 d6 3. d4 cxd4 4. Nxd4 Nf6 5. Nc3 a6 6. Bg5 Nbd7 7. f4 Qb6 8. a3 Qxb2

9. Na4

and the queen is trapped!

How to avoid the trap

With the b2 pawn untouchable, 8... h6 followed by the central thrust 9... e5 offers Black good prospects.

20. A False Gift
□ ♕

1. e4 c5 2. Nf3 d6 3. d4 cxd4 4. Nxd4 Nf6 5. Bc4 Nxe4 6. Qh5 e6 (6... g6 7. Qd5) 7. Bb5+ Bd7 8. Nxe6 Qa5+ 9. Bd2 Nxd2

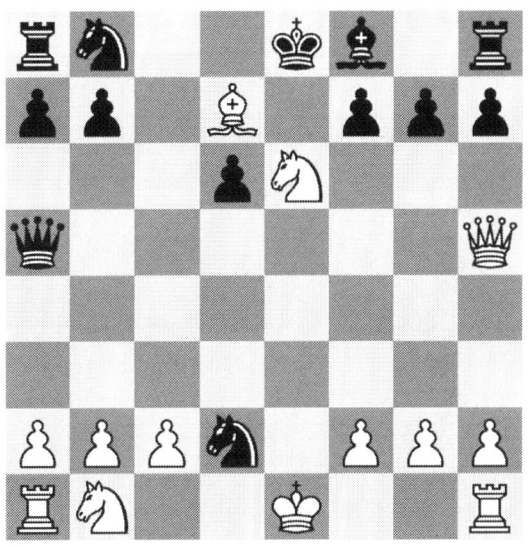

10. Bxd7+

and the black queen is lost.

How to avoid the trap

Instead, Black should have played 7... Nd7, and after 8. Nxe6 Nf6 9. Nxd8 Nxh5 10. Bxd7+ Bxd7 11. Nxb7 Bc6, Black recovers the g2 pawn. Note that after 7... Bd7 8. Nxe6 Qf6, the fork on c7 leads to nothing due to the mate threat on f2.

21. The Non-Capture on d4
□ ♝/♞

1. e4 c5 2. Nf3 e6 3. d4 Nc6?

4. d5

exd5 5. exd5 Nce7 6. d6 Nf5 7. Qe2+ Be7 8. dxe7

How to avoid the trap

Black must exchange in the center with 3... cxd4 to block the advance of White's central pawns.

22. The Tempting Pawn

1. e4 c5 2. Nf3 d6 3. c3 Nf6 4. Be2 Nxe4?

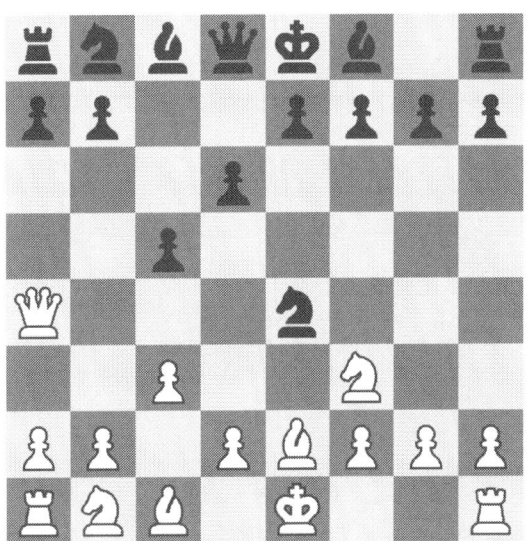

5. Qa4+

and the knight is lost.

How to avoid the trap

Black must avoid trying to win the e4 pawn and instead focus on development, for example with 4... Nc6. However, care must be taken not to fall into another trap after 5. d4 Nxe4? 6. d5! If the Nc6 moves, the check on a4 spells the end for the Ne4. After 5. d4 cxd4 6. cxd4, the move 6... Nxe4 is playable (although e6 is preferable) because after 7. d5, Black has time to insert 7... Qa5+.

23. A Troublesome Knight
□ #

1. e4 c5 2. Nf3 Nc6 3. d4 cxd4 4. Nxd4 Nf6 5. Nc3 e5 6. Ndb5 d6 7. Nd5 Nxd5 8. exd5 Ne7 9. c4 a6

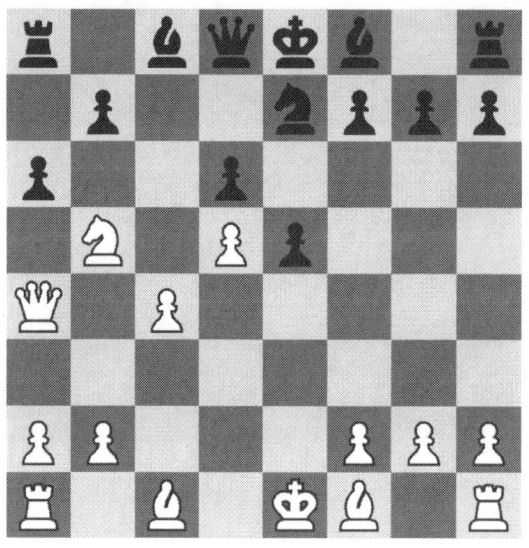

10. Qa4

Bd7 11. Nxd6#

How to avoid the trap

Black needs to give their king some breathing room by repositioning the Ne7, for instance with 9... Ng6. Now 10. Qa4 Bd7 becomes possible because the d6 pawn is defended. Note that 10... Qd7 11. Nxd6+ Kd8 12. Nxf7+ Ke8 13. Qxd7+ Bxd7 14. Nxh8 gives White a significant material advantage.

24. A Hole in the Defense
□ ♜

1. e4 c5 2. Nf3 Nc6 3. d4 cxd4 4. Nxd4 g6 5. Nc3 Bg7 6. Be3 a6?

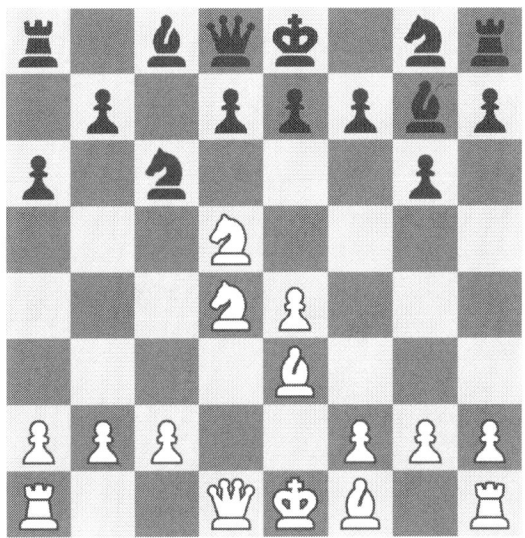

7. Nd5

e6? 8. Nxc6 bxc6 9. Bb6 Qh4 10. Nc7+ Kf8 11. Bc5+ Ne7 12. Nxa8 Qxe4+ 13. Qe2

How to avoid the trap

While the move a6 is often played by Black in the Sicilian, it is not good here because it grants White access to the b6 square. After 6... Nf6 7. Bc4 O-O 8. Bb3 Re8, the battle for control of the center continues with equal chances.

25. A Surprising Gambit

☐ ♖/♘

1. e4 c5 2. b4 cxb4 3. d4 Nc6 4. d5 Ne5 5. Bb2 d6 6. Nf3 Bg4?

7. Nxe5

Bxd1 8. Bb5+ Qd7 9. Bxd7+ Kd8 10. Nxf7+ Kxd7 11. Kxd1 Nf6 12. Nxh8

With precise play, it is not out of the question for White to maintain the knight on h8.

How to avoid the trap

After 6... Nf6 7. Nxe5 dxe5 8. Bb5+ Bd7 9. Bxd7+ Nxd7, Black has good practical chances. They will aim to exploit the opening of the c-file, and the b4 pawn could become a problem for White.

26. A French Variation

■ ♙

1. e4 c5 2. Nf3 e6 3. d4 cxd4 4. Nxd4 Nf6 5. e5?

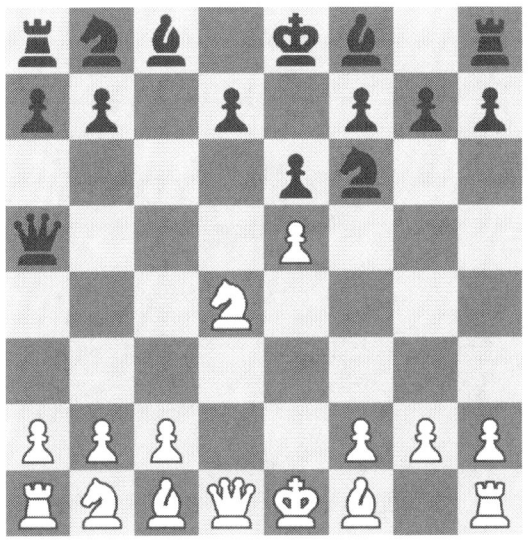

5... Qa5+

6. Nc3 Qxe5+

How to avoid the trap

White does better to play 5. Nc3, which develops a piece and prevents any check from the Black queen on a5. The game is currently equal.

27. A Trap Against the Grand Prix Attack
■ ♗/W-

1. e4 c5 2. Nc3 Nc6 3. f4 g6 4. Nf3 Bg7 5. Bc4 e6 6. O-O Nge7 7. d3 O-O 8. Qe1 d5 9. Bb3 Na5 10. Ne2?

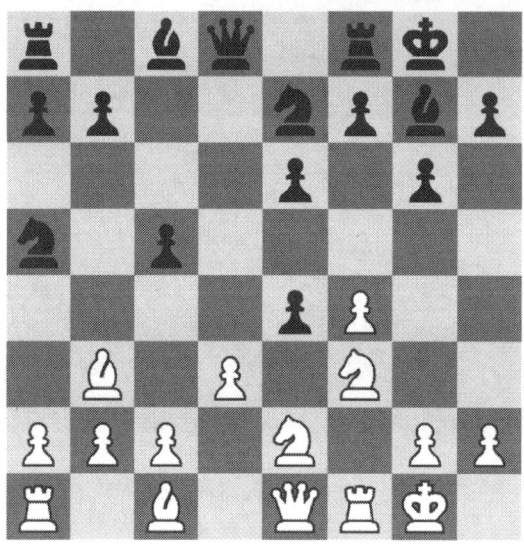

10... dxe4

11. dxe4 c4 12. Bd2 Nec6 13. Ba4 b5 14. Bxb5 Qb6+

(If 14. b4, then 14... cxb3 15. Bxb3 Bxa1 16. Qxa1 follows.)

How to avoid the trap

By attempting to reposition their Nc3 on the 10th move, White allows Black access to the c4 square after central pawn exchanges on e4. It is better to play 10. Bd2, leaving Black with no issues.

28. The Siberian Trap
■ #/♛

1. e4 c5 2. d4 cxd4 3. c3 dxc3 4. Nxc3 Nc6 5. Nf3 e6 6. Bc4 Qc7 7. O-O Nf6 8. Qe2 Ng4! 9. h3??

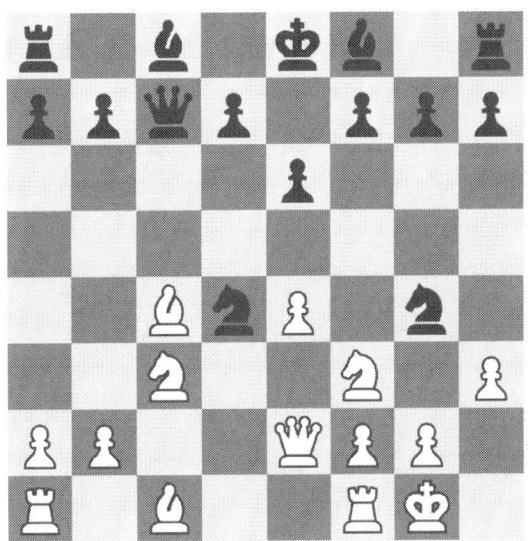

9... Nd4!

10. Nxd4 (10. hxg4 Nxe2+ ; 10. Qd1 Nxf3+ 11. Qxf3 Qh2#) 10... Qh2#

How to avoid the trap

The move 9. h3, which allows the black knight access to d4, loses immediately. Here, White must play 9. Nb5 to force the Black queen back to b8 (all other moves allow 10. Bf4 with a strong White attack) before driving away the knight with 10. h3

29. Another Trap in the Smith-Morra Gambit

1. e4 c5 2. d4 cxd4 3. c3 dxc3 4. Nxc3 e6 5. Nf3 Bb4 6. Bc4 Qc7 7. Qe2?

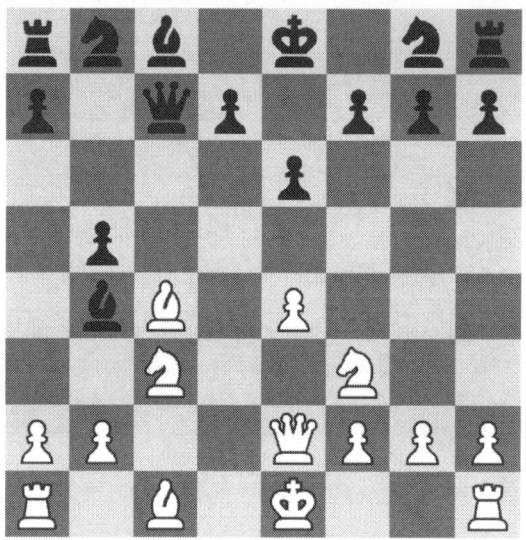

7... b5

8. Bxb5 Bxc3+ 9. bxc3 Qxc3+ 10. Qd2 Qxa1

How to avoid the trap

After 5... Bf4, White can play 6. Qd4, targeting both g7 and the Bb4. Since retreating the bishop to f8 isn't very appealing, Black often plays 6... Bxc3+, and after 7. bxc3 Nf6 8. e5 Nc6 9. Qf4, the chances are equal.

The French Defense

The French Defense begins with the moves 1. e4 e6

30. Chernev's Greek Gift
☐ #

1. e4 e6 2. d4 d5 3. Nc3 Nf6 4. Bg5 Be7 5. e5 Ne4 6. Bxe7 Qxe7 7. Qg4 O-O? 8. Bd3 Nxc3 9. bxc3 c5 10. Nf3 c4?

11. Bxh7+

Kxh7 12. Qh5+ Kg8 13. Ng5 Rd8 14. Qh7+ Kf8 15. Qh8#

How to avoid the trap

Black should have counterattacked with 7... Qb4, and after 8. Qxg7 Rf8 9. Rd1 Nxc3 10. bxc3 Qxc3+, the position is equal.

31. Queen in Check
□ ♛

1. e4 e6 2. d4 d5 3. e5 c5 4. c3 Nc6 5. Nf3 Qb6 6. Bd3 cxd4 7. cxd4 Nxd4

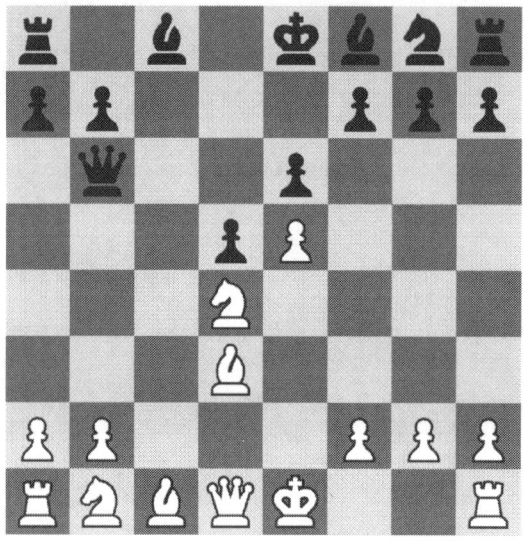

8. Nxd4

Qxd4 9. Bb5+, and the queen is lost 9... Bd7 10. Bxd7+ Kxd7 11. Qxd4

How to avoid the trap

Black must absolutely shield their king from the check with 7... Bd7 before thinking of capturing the d4 pawn!

32. Fatal Fork
□ ♖ / ♗

1. e4 e6 2. d4 d5 3. exd5 exd5 4. c4 Nf6 5. Nc3 Bb4 6. Nf3 O-O 7. Bd3 Re8+ 8. Be3 Ng4 9. O-O Nxe3 10. fxe3 Rxe3

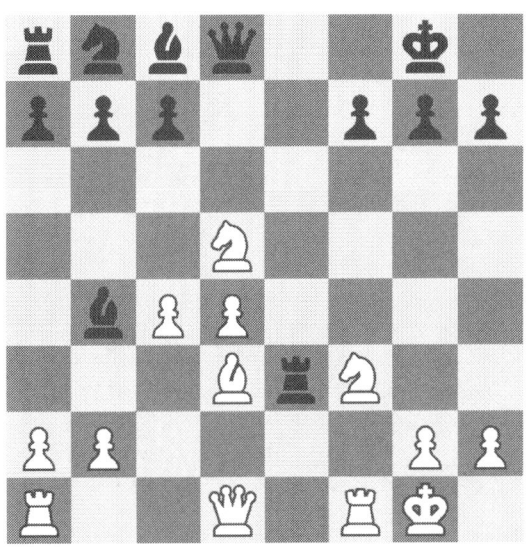

11. Nxd5

How to avoid the trap

Black is too greedy by trying to capture the e3 pawn while their pieces are poorly placed. 8... Bg4 9. O-O c6 followed by Nbd7 ensures them good chances to equalize thanks to a solid center.

33. Two's Company
□#

1. e4 e6 2. d4 d5 3. Nc3 Bb4 4. exd5 Bxc3+ 5. bxc3 exd5 6. Nf3 Nf6 7. Ba3 Be6 8. Bb5+ c6 9. Bd3 Nbd7 10. Qe2 (threatening 10... Ng5) h6

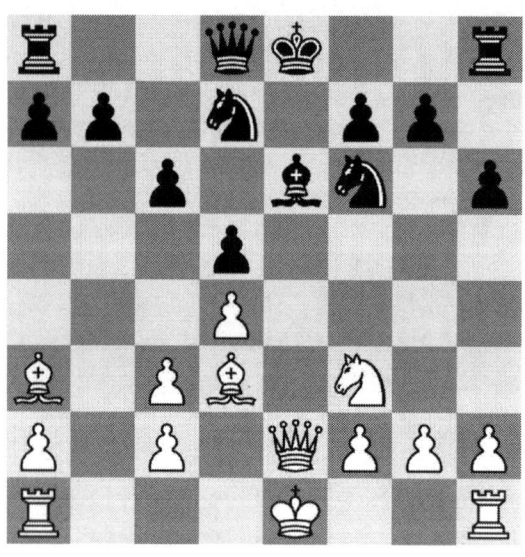

11. Qxe6+ !

11... fxe6 12. Bg6#

How to avoid the trap

Several imprecise moves by Black in this game, but the decisive mistake is, of course, 10... h6, which creates weaknesses and allows a combination. The correct move was 10... c5, and after 11. dxc5 O-O 12. O-O Bg4, Black has active play that compensates for the pawn, as White's tripled pawns are weak.

34. Morphy's Trap

■ ♛

McConnell - Morphy 1850 : 1. e4 e6 2. d4 d5 3. e5 c5 4. c3 Nc6 5. f4 Qb6 6. Nf3 Bd7 7. a3 Nh6 8. b4 cxd4 9. cxd4 Rc8 10. Bb2 Nf5 11. Qd3

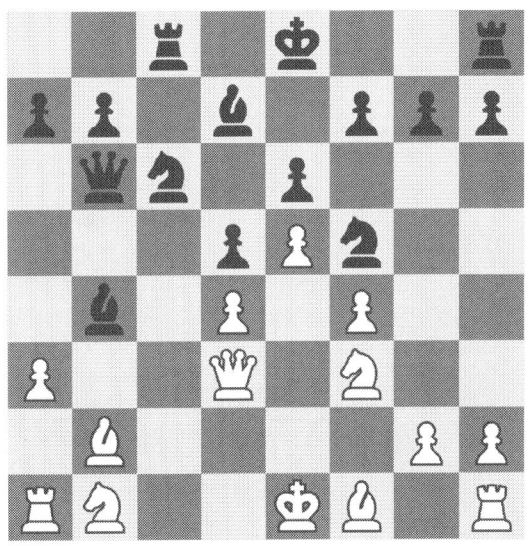

11... Bxb4+

12. axb4 Nxb4 13. Qd2 Rc2 14. Qd1 Ne3

How to avoid the trap

There are many inaccuracies in this historic game, but the main mistake by White is 11. Qd3, which allows the combination leading to the loss of the queen. They should have played 11. Qd2, keeping equal chances.

35. The Tables Turned

■ #

1. e4 e6 2. d4 d5 3. Nc3 Bb4 4. Ne2 dxe4 5. a3 Be7 6. Nxe4 Nd7 7. Nf4 Ngf6 8. Ng5 O-O 9. Ngxe6 fxe6 10. Nxe6 Qe8 11. Nxc7??

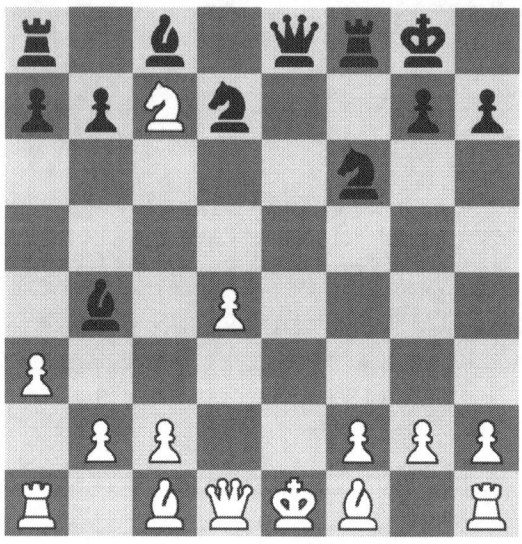

11... Bb4#

How to avoid the trap

The sacrifice 9. Ngxe6 is sound, but White is too greedy in taking the c7 pawn. Note that 11. Nxf8 meets the same fate. A possible continuation is 11. Bc4 Bd6 12. O-O Kh8 13. Re1 Nb6 14. Nxf8 Qxf8, with equal chances.

The Caro-Kann Defense

The Caro-Kann Defense begins with the moves 1. e4 c6

36. The Anand-Carlsen Theme
☐ B-

1. e4 c6 2. d4 d5 3. Nc3 dxe4 4. Nxe4 Bf5 5. Ng3 Bg6 6. h4 h6 7. Nf3 e6 8. Ne5 Bh7 9. Bd3 Qxd4?

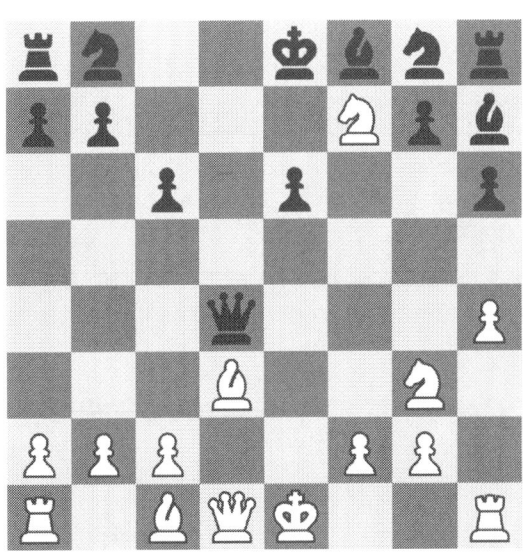

10. Nxf7

Bxd3 11. Nxh8 Qe5+ 12. Be3 Bh7 13. Qd8+ Kxd8 14. Nf7+

How to avoid the trap

The d4 pawn cannot be captured. Black is better off simply accepting the exchange of light-squared bishops with 9... Bxd3, and after 10. Qxd3 Nd7 11. f4 Be7 12. Bd2 Nxe5 13. fxe5 Bxh4, the position is completely equal.

37. Mate in 6 Moves!
□ #

1. e4 c6 2. d4 d5 3. Nc3 dxe4 4. Nxe4 Nd7 5. Qe2 Ngf6

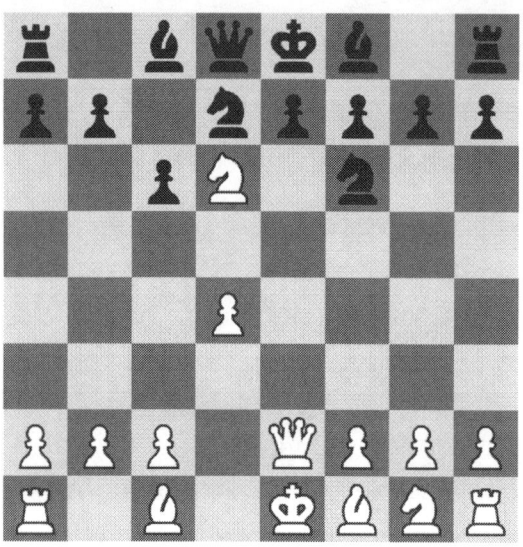

6. Nd6#

How to avoid the trap

Although 4... Nd7 is perfectly playable, caution is needed, especially in blitz games, because the common continuation is 5. Nf3, to which Black often responds immediately with 5... Ngf6. Against 5. Qe2, it's best to play 5... Ndf6, and Black is doing well.

38. A Quality Trap
☐ B-

1. e4 c6 2. d4 d5 3. f3 dxe4 4. fxe4 e5 5. Nf3 exd4 6. Bc4 Nf6 7. O-O Bc5 8. Ng5 O-O

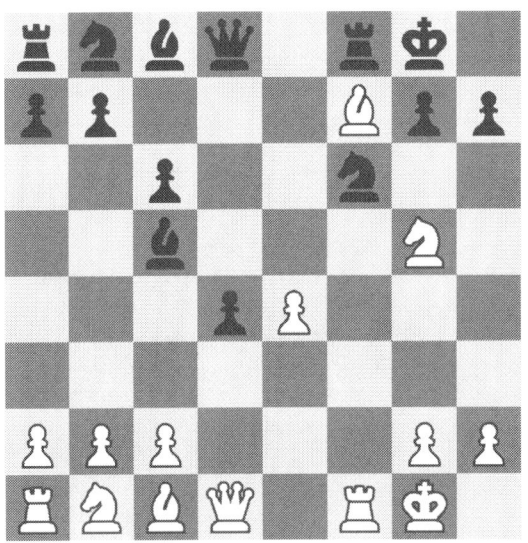

9. Bxf7+

Rxf7 10. Nxf7 Kxf7 11. Qh5+ Kg8 12. Qxc5

How to avoid the trap

It's better to pin the knight with 5... Bg4. After 6. Bc4, the d4 pawn cannot be captured because of 7. Bxf7+ Kxf7 8. Ne5+ Ke8 9. Qxg4, leaving Black in a catastrophic position. After 6... Nd7 7. O-O Ngf6 8. c3 Bd6, Black will be able to castle into an equal position.

39. Bishops on the File

■ ♝

1. e4 c6 2. c4, rare but playable, d5 3. exd5 cxd5 4. cxd5 Nf6 5. Bb5+ Bd7 6. Bc4 Qc7 7. Qb3 (White is threatening f7 after d6) but...

7... b5!

and one of the bishops is lost.

How to avoid the trap

7. d3 b5 and the bishop has a retreat square with 8. Bb3

The Scotch Game

The Scotch Game begins with the moves 1. e4 e5 2. Nf3 Nc6 3. d4

40. A Stranded Bishop

1. e4 e5 2. Nf3 Nc6 3. d4 exd4 4. Nxd4 Bc5 5. Be3 Nf6

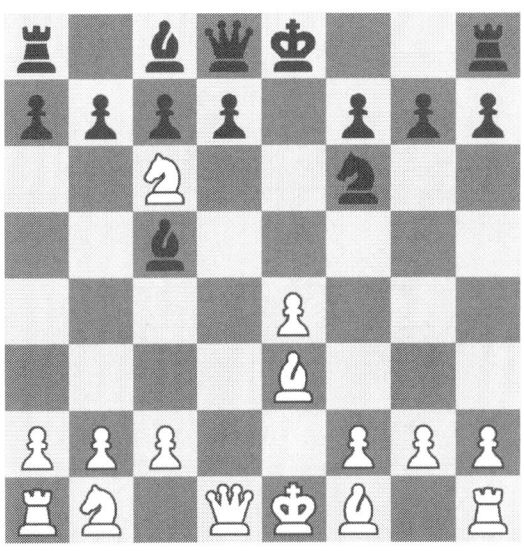

6. Nxc6

dxc6 7. Qxd8+ Kxd8 8. Bxc5 Nxe4

How to avoid the trap

On move 5, Black can exchange knights or play the main line with 5... Qf6. Now 6. Nxc6 is no longer good because the queen is no longer on d8: 6. Nxc6 Bxe3 7. fxe3 dxc6, and White finds themselves burdened with doubled central pawns.

41. The Nd2 Trap

□ ♝

1. e4 e5 2. Nf3 Nc6 3. d4 exd4 4. Nxd4 Bc5 5. Be3 Qf6 6. c3 Nge7 7. Nd2 Nxd4 8. e5 Qxe5?

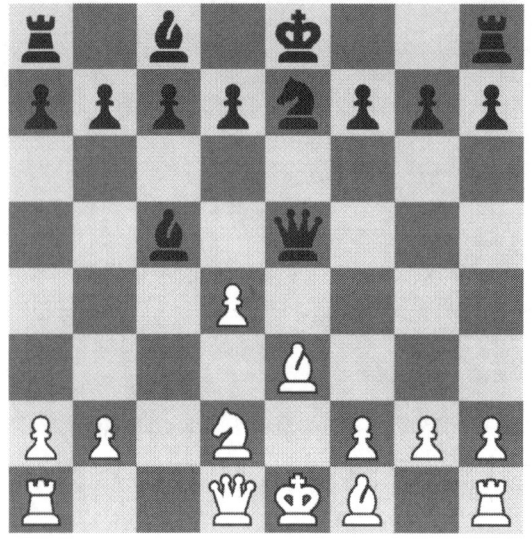

9. cxd4

Bxd4 10. Nc4!

How to avoid the trap

The correct move for Black is 8... Nc2+ 9. Qxc2 Qxe5, which leaves them with a slight advantage. Note that the move 8... Qxe5 is played 85% of the time!

42. Quick Mate
□ #

1. e4 e5 2. Nf3 Nc6 3. d4 exd4 4. Ng5 h6 5. Nxf7 Kxf7 6. Bc4+ Ke8

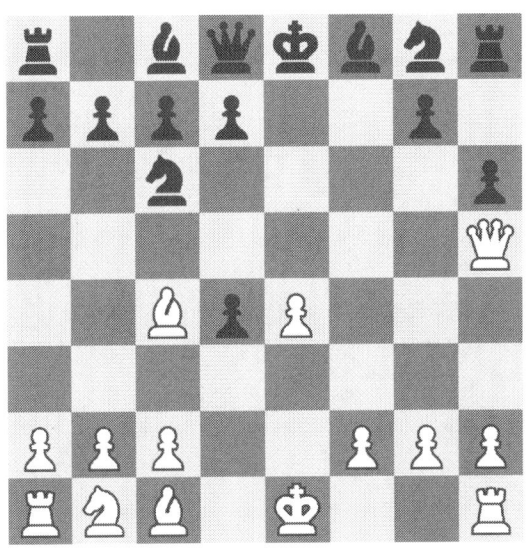

7. Qh5+

Ke7 8. Qf7+ Kd6 9. e5+ Nxe5 (9... Kxe5 10. Qf4#) (9... Kc5 10. Qd5+ Kb6 11. Qb5#) 10. Qd5+ Ke7 11. Qxe5#

How to avoid the trap

Approximately 52% of players play 6... Ke8, which loses immediately. The correct move is the counterintuitive 6... Kg6, because after 7. Qg4+ Kh7 8. Qf5+ g6 9. Qf7+ Bg7, White has no more threats. However, the best solution is still 4... Be7, forcing White to retreat without compensation for the pawn.

43. A Overpowering Pawn

■ ♜

1. e4 e5 2. Nf3 Nc6 3. d4 exd4 4. Bc4 Be7 5. c3 dxc3 6. Qd5 Nh6 7. Bxh6 O-O 8. Bc1

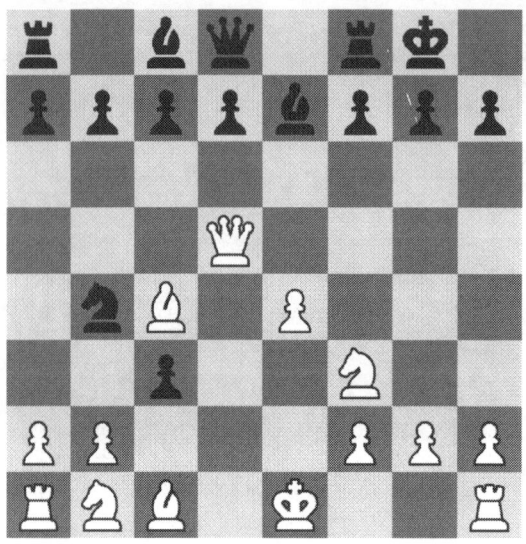

8... Nb4

9. Qd1 c2 10. Qe2 cxb1=Q 11. Rxb1 d5 12. exd5 Bf5 and if 13. Ra1 Nc2+

How to avoid the trap

Surprisingly, White must give back the piece with 8. Bxg7 because the Black pawn on c3 is too strong. After 8... Kxg7 9. Nxc3 d6 10. Qh5 f5 11. O-O fxe4 12. Nxe4 Qe8, Black has little to fear despite the apparent exposure of their king.

The Göring Gambit

The Göring Gambit begins with the moves 1. e4 e5 2. Nf3 Nc6 3. d4 exd4 4. c3

44. The Gunner Bishop
□

1. e4 e5 2. Nf3 Nc6 3. d4 exd4 4. c3 dxc3 5. Nxc3 Bb4 6. Bc4 Bxc3+ 7. bxc3 d6 8. Qb3 Qe7 9. O-O Nf6 10. e5 dxe5

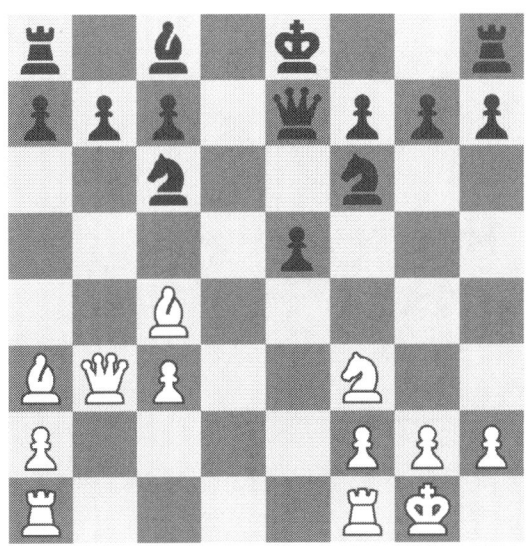

11. Ba3

Qd7 12. Rad1 Na5 13. Rxd7 Nxb3 14. Re7+ Kd8 15. Bxb3

How to avoid the trap

Black seems to play natural moves up to move 11. However, they must recapture with the knight: 10... Nxe5 11. Nxe5 dxe5 12. Ba3 c5! and now it is Black who has a slight advantage.

The Three Knights Game

The Three Knights Game begins with the moves 1. e4 e5 2. Nf3 Nc6 3. Nc3 without 3... Nf6

45. Winning Combo
□ #

1. e4 e5 2. Nf3 Nc6 3. Nc3 g6 4. d4 exd4 5. Nd5 Bg7 6. Bg5 Nge7?

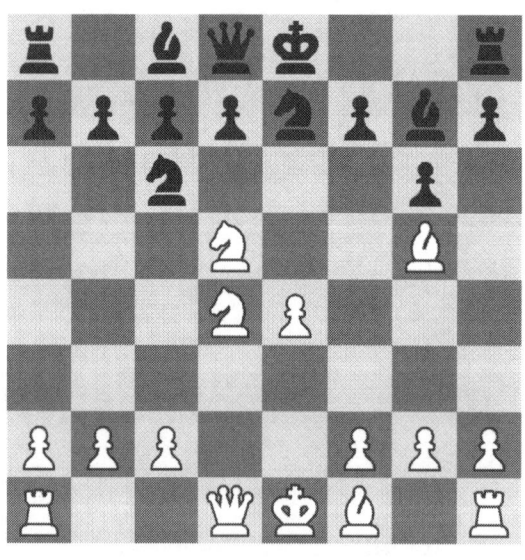

7. Nxd4

Bxd4 8. Qxd4 Nxd4 9. Nf6+ Kf8 10. Bh6#

How to avoid the trap

6... Nce7 sacrifices the pawn but safely protects the queen: 7. Nxd4 c6 8. Nxe7 Nxe7 9. Qd2 h6, and Bg5 must retreat.

The Russian Defense or Petrov

The Petrov Defense begins with the moves 1.e4 e5 2.Nf3 Nf6

46. A Bad Pin

1. e4 e5 2. Nf3 Nf6 3. Nxe5 d6 4. Nf3 Nxe4 5. Qe2 Qe7 6. d3 Nf6 7. Be3 Nc6 8. Nc3 Bg4 9. h3 Bh5 10. g4 Bg6 11. g5 Nd7

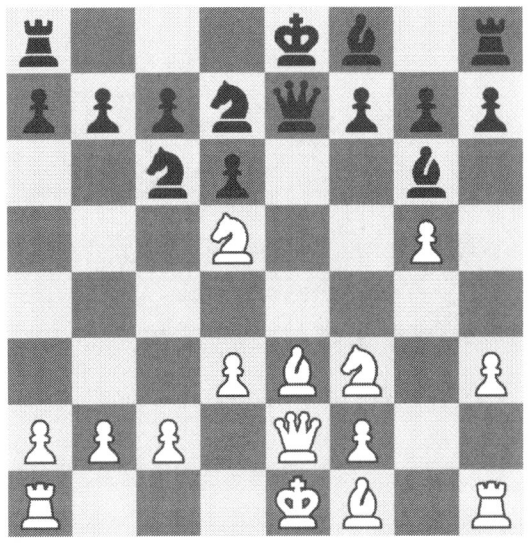

12. Nd5

Qd8 13. Nxc7+ Qxc7 14. Bb6+

How to avoid the trap : The pin with 8... Bg4 is not yet a mistake but sets the stage for a trap. 8... d5 is preferable, as it gives Black some breathing room and prepares queenside castling after, for example, Bf5. The decisive mistake is retreating the Nf6 to d7. They should have minimized the damage with 11... Ng8 and later Ne7.

47. The Stafford Gambit Trap

1. e4 e5 2. Nf3 Nf6 3. Nxe5 Nc6 4. Nxc6 dxc6 5. e5 Ne4 6. d3

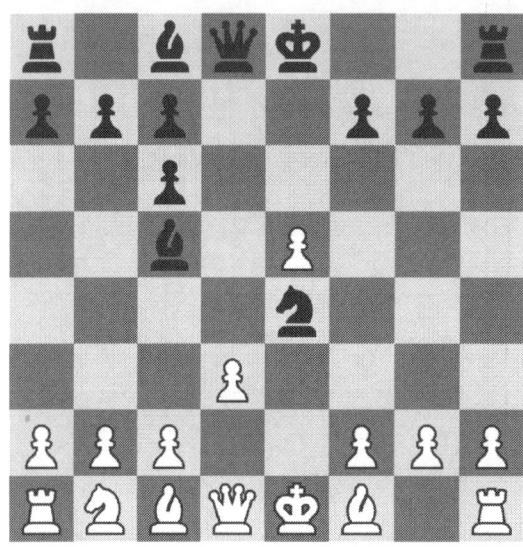

6... Bc5

7. dxe4 Bxf2+ 8. Kxf2 Qxd1

How to avoid the trap

With the knight on e4, Black must absolutely prevent Bc5, targeting f2, by playing 6. d4! After 6. d3 Bc5, 7. Be3 doesn't work due to 7... Bxe3 8. fxe3 Qh4+ 9. g3 Nxg3 10. hxg3 Qxh1

The Philidor Defense

The Philidor Defense begins with the moves 1. e4 e5 2. Nf3 e6

48. The Famous f7 Square

1. e4 e5 2. Nf3 d6 3. Bc4 Nf6 4. Nc3 Nbd7 5. Ng5 Qe7

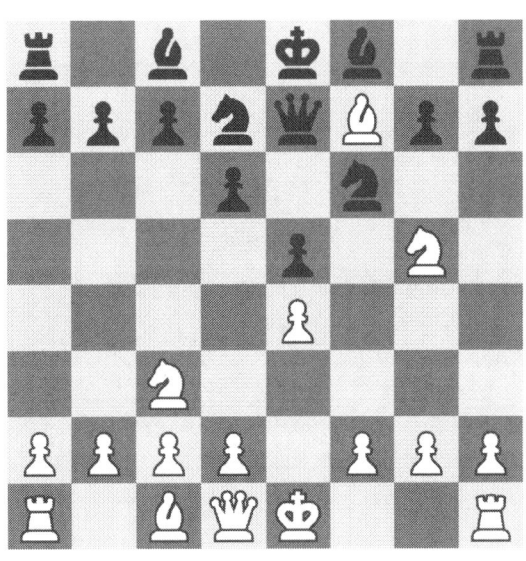

6. Bxf7+

Kd8 7. Ne6+ Qxe6 8. Bxe6

How to avoid the trap

Following 5. Ng5, Black can play 5... d5, and after 6. exd5 Nb6 7. d3 Bb4 8. O-O Nxc4 9. dxc4 Bxc3 10. bxc3 O-O, White has a pawn advantage but also tripled pawns. The chances are equal.

49. Don't Play Passively!
□ #/♞

1. e4 e5 2. Nf3 d6 3. d4 Nd7 4. Bc4 Be7 5. dxe5 dxe5 6. Qd5 Nh6 7. Bxh6

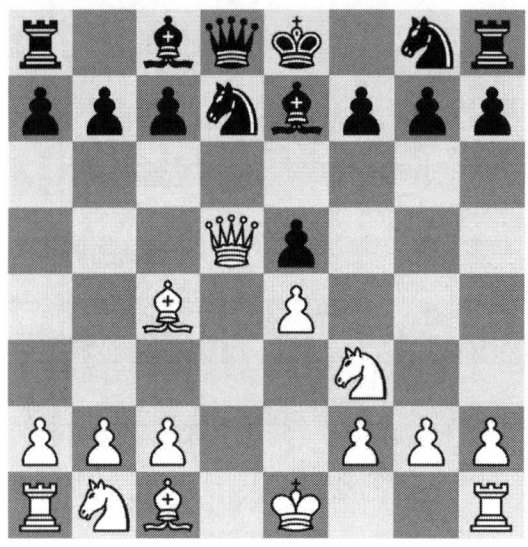

6. Qd5

6... Nh6 7. Bxh6

How to avoid the trap

4... Be7 to prevent 5. Ng5 is a mistake. The correct move is 4... exd4 5. Qxd4 Ngf6, and in response to 6. Ng5, Ne5 covers f7 and repels White's attack.

The Ponziani Opening

The Ponziani Opening begins with the moves 1.e4 e5 2.Nf3 Nc6 3.c3

50. The Flagship Trap
□ #

1. e4 e5 2. Nf3 Nc6 3. c3 Nf6 4. d4 Nxe4 5. d5 Ne7 6. Nxe5 Ng6 7. Bd3. White offers the exchange of a minor piece. Here, Black might be tempted to win a pawn with 7... Nxf2?, but then...

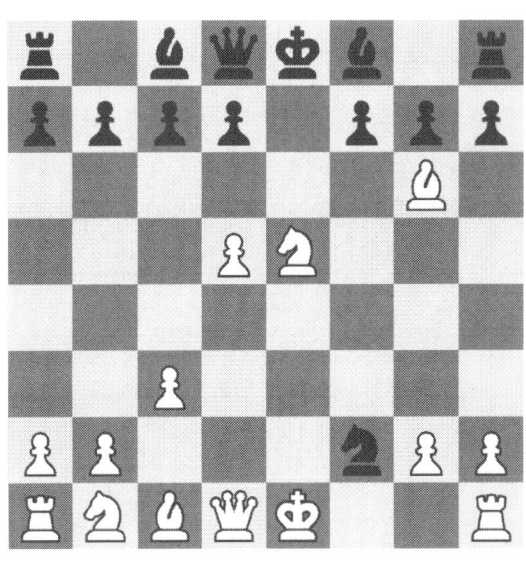

8. Bxg6!

If Black captures the queen, 8... Nxd1 9. Bxf7+ Ke7 10. Bg5+ Kd6 11. Nc4+ Kc5. White can now either recapture the queen or try 12. Nba3, and if 12... Qxg5, then 13. b4#

How to avoid the trap

After the central exchange 7... Nxe5 8. Bxe4 Bc5, Black no longer has any problems.

The Vienna Game

The Vienna Game begins with the moves 1. e4 e5 2. Nc3

51. A Beautiful Mate
□ #

1. e4 e5 2. Nc3 Nf6 3. Bc4 Nxe4 4. Bxf7+ (4. Nxe4 d5) Kxf7 5. Nxe4 d6? (5... d5!) 6. Qf3+ Kg8?

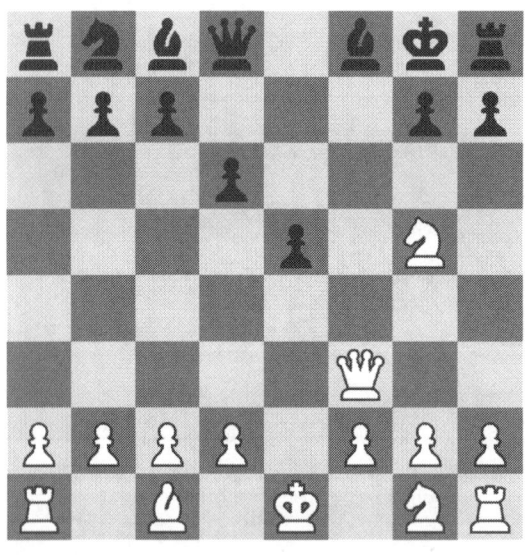

7. Ng5

Qxg5?? 8. Qd5+ Be6 9. Qxe6#

How to avoid the trap

Even though it's better for Black to play aggressively with 5... d5, they can still limit the damage with 6... Ke8. The king is displaced, but Black has the bishop pair and a strong central pawn on e5.

52. The Queen Steps Out
□ #

1. e4 e5 2. Nc3 Nc6 3. Bc4 Bc5

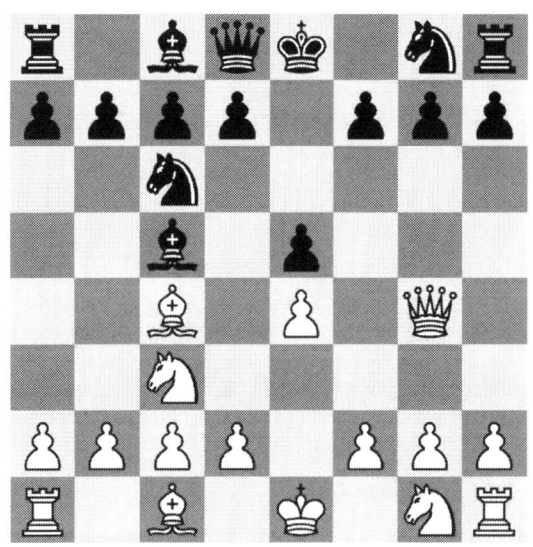

4. Qg4

4... Nf6 ?? 5. Qxg7 Rg8
6. Qxf7#

How to avoid the trap

Black has realized that after 4... Qf6, they face problems due to 5. Nd5 (attacking the queen and threatening 6... Nxc7), and they don't want to displace their king with 4... Kf8. However, they are wrong because it's the correct move! Indeed, after 5. Qg3 (to block 5... d5!) Nf6, the queen is exposed, and moves like Nh5 or h5 become threatening.

The Bishop's Opening

The Bishop's Opening begins with the moves 1. e4 e5 2. Bc4

53. Fatal Assault
□ #

1. e4 e5 2. Bc4 Nf6 3. Nc3 Bc5 4. d3 d6 5. f4 Ng4 6. f5 Nf2

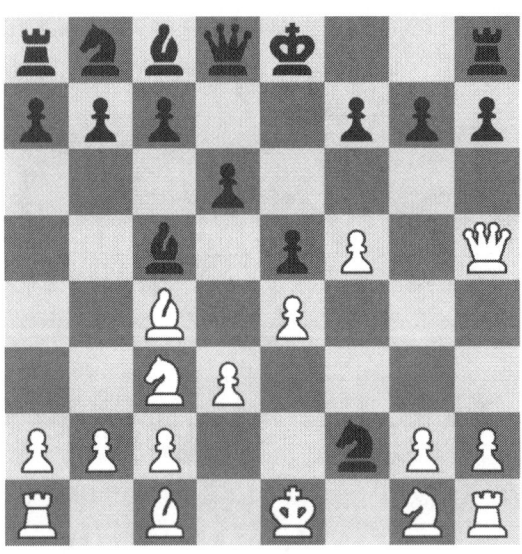

7. Qh5

7... O-O 8. Bg5 Qe8 9. Nd5 Nxh1 10. Nf6+ gxf6 11. Bxf6, and Black is powerless to stop the queen from delivering mate on the g-file.

How to avoid the trap

6... h5 defends the Ng4 and sets a trap: if White wants to challenge it with 7. h3, then 7... Qh4+ 8. g3 Qxg3+ 9. Kf1 Qf2# follows.

54. Queen Exchange
□ ♙ ♙

1. e4 e5 2. Bc4 Nc6 3. Qh5 g6 4. Qf3 Nf6 5. Ne2 Bg7 6. Nbc3 O-O 7. d3 d6 8. Bg5 Bg4 9. Bxf6 Bxf3?

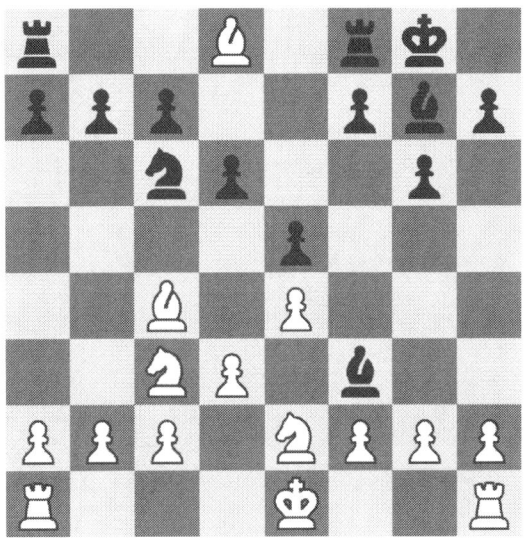

10. Bxd8

Bxe2 11. Bxc7 Bg4 12. Bxd6 Rfd8 13. Bc5

How to avoid the trap

The moves presented for Black are the most commonly played starting from move 3 in the database! There are no major mistakes until 9... Bxf3. The move here should be 9... Qd7, and after 10. Qg3, Black can recover the f6 bishop, reaching an equal position.

The Center Game

The Center Game begins with the moves 1.e4 e5 2.d4 exd4 3.Qxd4

55. Goodbye, Madam!

1. e4 e5 2. d4 exd4 3. Qxd4 Nc6 4. Qa4 Nf6 5. Nc3 d5 6. Bg5 dxe4 7. Nxe4 Qe7 8. O-O-O Qxe4?

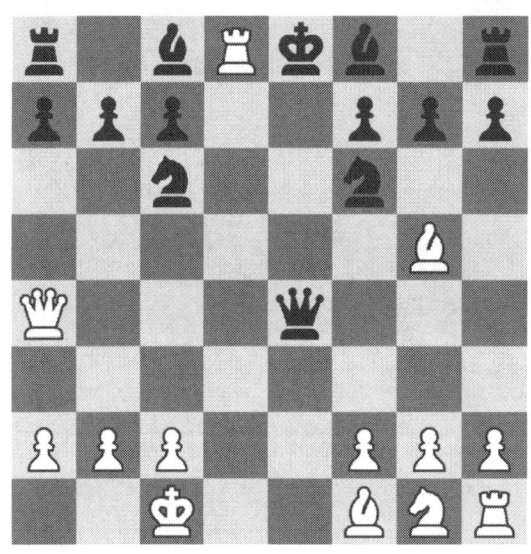

9. Rd8+

Kxd8 10. Bxf6+ gxf6 11. Qxe4

How to avoid the trap

7... Qe7 is a natural move aiming to take advantage of the pin on Ne4, but 7... Bb4+ or Be7 are better. The blunder, of course, is 8... Qxe4. Instead, Black should play 8... Bd7, and after 9. Nxf6+ gxf6 10. Be3, Black can plan to castle queenside.

The Danish Gambit

The Danish Gambit begins with the moves 1. e4 e5 2. d4 exd4 3. c3

56. Queen in the Center
□ ±

1.e4 e5 2.d4 exd4 3.c3 dxc3 4.Nxc3 Bb4 5.Bc4 Nf6 6.e5 Ne4?

7.Qd5

The simultaneous attack on f7 and the Ne4 gives White a significant advantage.

How to avoid the trap

The premature development of Nf6 is a mistake that allows the e-pawn to advance. After 5... Bxc3+ 6. bxc3 Qe7, Black isolates White's c-pawn and maintains central pressure, resulting in an equal position.

57. The Danish Bird Trap
■ ∓

1. e4 e5 2. d4 exd4 3. c3 dxc3 4. Bc4 cxb2 5. Bxb2

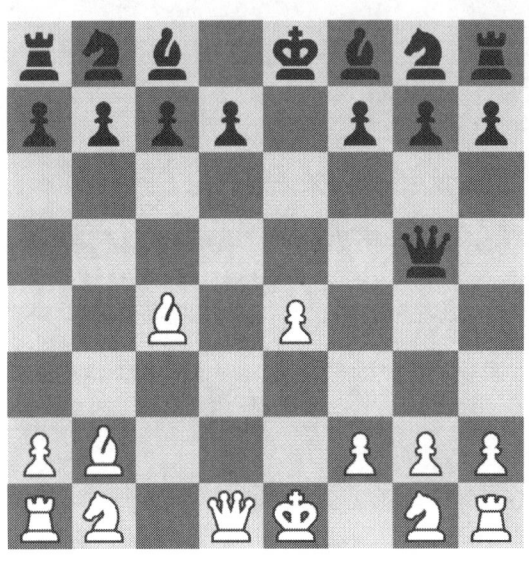

5... Qg5

White has sacrificed two pawns in the opening and must absolutely keep the initiative. With this move, Black tries to seize it back by counterattacking. If White tries to defend g2 with 6. Qf3, then 6... d5! and Black is already better. 6. g3 Bb4+ equalizes, and 6. Qb3, which threatens f7, brings nothing because after 6... Qxg2 7. Bxf7+ Kd8 8. Qf3 Qxf3 9. Nxf3, Black is simply two pawns up.

How to avoid the trap

White should not worry about the g2 pawn. Instead, 6. Nf3! and after 6... Qxg2 7. Rg1 Qh3 8. Bxf7+ Kd8 9. Rxg7 Bxg7 10. Bxg7, Black can already resign.

The King's Gambit

The King's Gambit begins with the moves 1. e4 e5 2. f4

58. Queen or Mate?
□ ♕/#

1. e4 e5 2. f4 Bc5 3. Nf3 d6 4. c3 Qe7 5. d4 exd4 6. cxd4 Qxe4+?

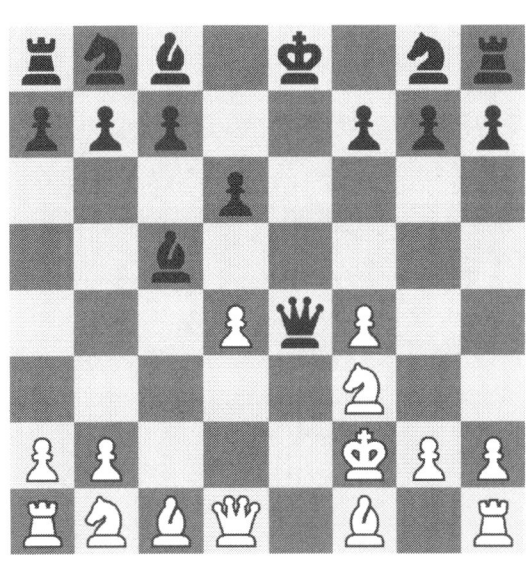

7. Kf2

After Bb6, 8. Bb5+ c6 9. Re1, the queen is lost. If 8... Kd8, then 9. Re1, and the queen cannot escape without allowing 10. Re8#

How to avoid the trap

Black must play 6... Bb6 and continue their development.

59. Quick Mate

□ #

1. e4 e5 2. f4 exf4 3. Nf3 g5 4. Nc3 g4 5. Ne5 Qh4+ 6. g3 fxg3 7. Qxg4 g2+?

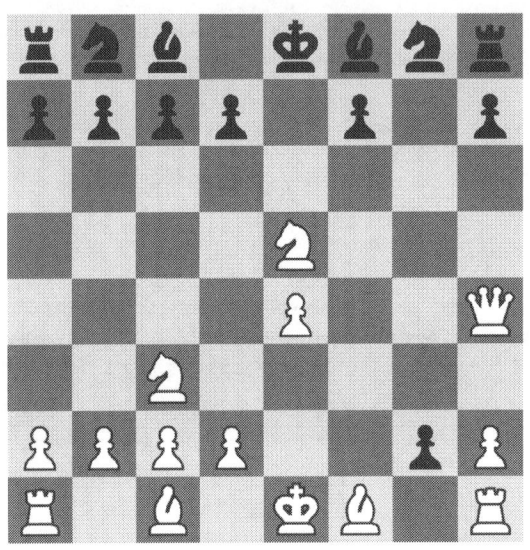

8. Qxh4

gxh1=Q 9. Qh5 Be7 10. Nxf7 Nf6 11. Nd6+ Kd8 12. Qe8+ Nxe8 13. Nf7#

How to avoid the trap

After 9... Nh6 10. d4 d6 11. Bxh6 dxe5 12. Be3!, Black may have an extra rook but will be forced to concede material. For example: 12... Bg7 13. O-O-O O-O 14. Bc4 Qg2 15. Rg1, and the queen is lost. Black can play 7... Qxg4 8. Nxg4 d5! (attacking Ng4), and the chances are equal.

60. A (Too) Greedy Queen
■ ♛

1. e4 e5 2. f4 d5 3. exd5 (3. fxe5 Qh4+ 4. g3 Qxe4+ loses immediately) c6 4. Qe2 cxd5 5. Qxe5+ Be7 6. Qxg7

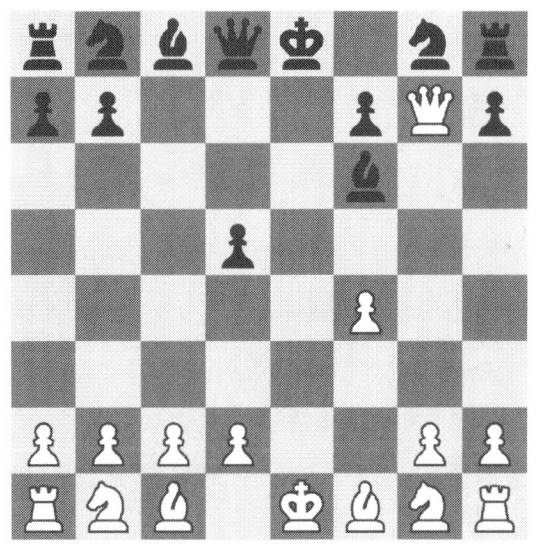

6... Bf6

7. Qg3 Bh4

How to avoid the trap

2... d5 is the Falkbeer Countergambit. After 6. Bb5+ Nc6 7. b3! (threatening Ba3) Nf6? (7... Be6!) 8. Bxc6+ bxc6 9. Ba3 Be6 10. Bxe7 Qxe7 11. Nf3 Nd7 12. Qxg7, White eventually captures the g7 pawn and secures an excellent position.

The Scandinavian Defense

The Scandinavian Defense begins with the moves 1. e4 d5

61. The Tennison Trap

1. e4 d5 2. Nf3 dxe4 3. Ng5 Nf6 4. d3 exd3 5. Bxd3 h6?

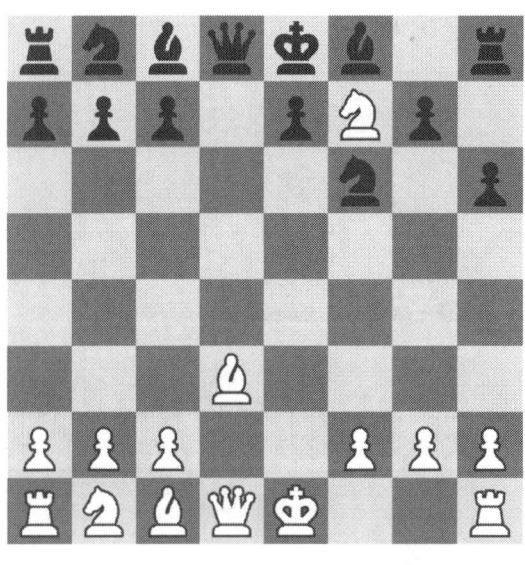

6. Nxf7

Kxf7 7. Bg6+ Kxg6 8. Qxd8

How to avoid the trap

Objectively, the Tennison Gambit favors Black, provided they play it correctly! Black can play 5... Nc6 to protect the queen, then 6... h6 without any issues.

62. Queen vs Queen
□ ♛

1. e4 d5 2. exd5 Qxd5 3. Nc3 Qa5 4. b4 Qxb4 5. Nb5 Qa5 6. Bc4 c6

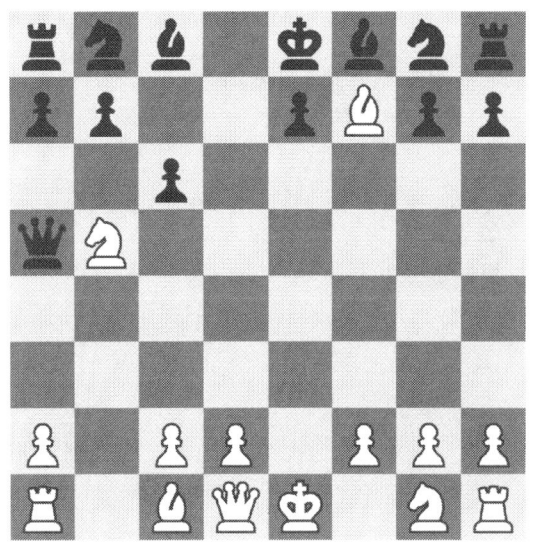

7. Bxf7+

Kxf7 8. Qh5+ g6 9. Nd6+ exd6 10. Qxa5

How to avoid the trap

After 6... Nc6! 7. a4 Nf6 8. Bb2 Bg4, White has no compensation for the sacrificed pawn.

63. Valencian Variation
□ #

1. e4 d5 2. exd5 Qxd5 3. Nc3 Qd8 4. Bc4 Nf6 5. Nf3 Bg4 ?

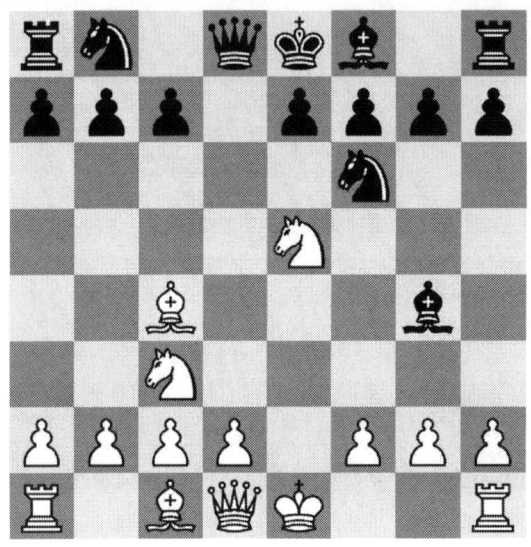

6. Ne5

Bxd1 ??

7. Bxf7#

How to avoid the trap

If they choose this line, Black must play carefully. 5... Bg5 6. d4 e6 7. d5 Bb4 8. dxe6 Bxe6 9. Bxe6 Bxc3+ 10. bxc3 Qxd1+ 11. Kxd1 fxe6 leads to an equal position.

64. Imperfect Pin

■ ♛

1. e4 d5 2. exd5 Nf6 3. d4 Nxd5 4. c4 Nb4 5. Qa4+ N8c6 6. a3 Na6 7. d5 Nc5 8. Qb5?

8... e6

9. dxc6 b6 10. Be3 a6 11. Qb4 Nd3+ 12. Bxd3 Bxb4+ 13. axb4 Qxd3

How to avoid the trap

White should not try to maintain the pin but instead retreat their queen with 8. Qd1. After 8... Ne5 9. b4 Ncd7 10. Bb2, White takes space on the queenside and gains an advantage because Black struggles to develop.

65. The Icelandic Gambit
■ #

1. e4 d5 2. exd5 Nf6 3. c4 e6 4. dxe6 Bxe6 5. d4 Bb4+ 6. Nc3 Ne4 7. Bd2

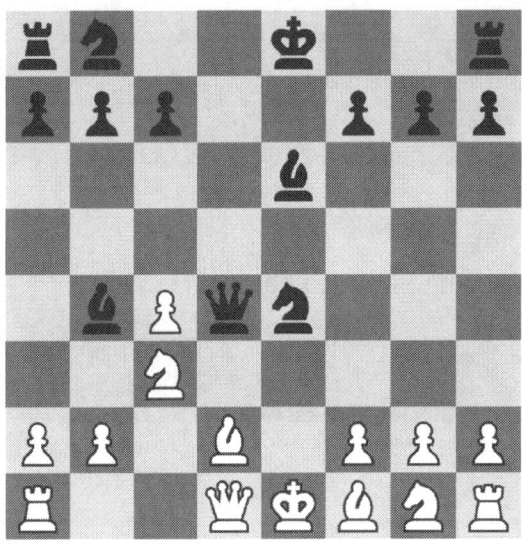

7... Qxd4

8. Nf3 Qxf2#

How to avoid the trap

White could have limited the damage after 8. Nxe4 Qxe4, even though Black's position is superior. White should have returned the pawn with 7. Ne2, although the best option is to return it from the start with 3. Nf3

The Pirc/Modern Defense

The Pirc Defense begins with the moves 1. e4 d6 2. d4 Nf6 3. Nc3 g6. The Modern Defense places the bishop on g7 without Nf6 (transpositions are common).

66. Fatal Retreat
□ #

1. e4 d6 2. d4 Nf6 3. Nc3 g6 4. Bf4 Bg7 5. e5 dxe5 6. dxe5 Qxd1+ 7. Rxd1 Nfd7 8. Nd5 Nxe5??

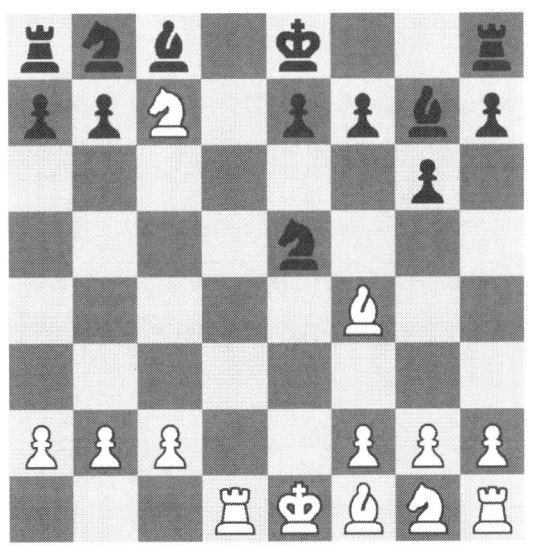

9. Nxc7+

Kf8 10. Rd8#

How to avoid the trap

lack must not back down from the e5 pawn. 5... Nh5 forces the Bf4 to retreat. For example: 6. Bg3 Nxg3 7. hxg3 dxe5 8. dxe5 Qxd1+ 9. Rxd1 Bxe5. Black is a pawn up and ready to castle.

67. The Suffocated Queen
□♛/#

1. e4 d6 2. d4 Nd7 3. Bc4 g6 4. Nf3 Bg7

5. Bxf7+

Kxf7 6. Ng5+ Ke8 (or Kf8) 7. Ne6

or

6... Kf6 7. Qf3#

How to avoid the trap

2... Nd7 is playable but traps the queen. After 3. Bc4, Black must counterattack in the center with 3... Ngf6 and then fianchetto their bishop before castling.

Alekhine Defense

The Alekhine Defense begins with the moves 1. e4 Nf6

68. A Strange King Move

1. e4 Nf6 2. e5 Nd5 3. d4 e6 4. c4 Bb4+

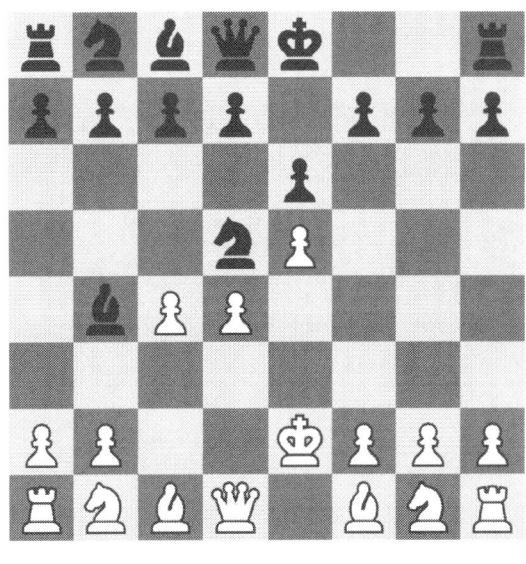

5. Ke2

5... Ne7 6. a3 Ba5 7. b4 Bb6 8. c5

or

5... Nb6 6. c5 Nc4 (6... Nd5 7. a3 Ba5 8. b4) 7. Qb3

How to avoid the trap

3... e6 is already not the best move (3... d6!), but 4... Bb4+ seals the bishop's fate. Strangely, in this position, only 1% of players have found the winning move 5. Ke2!

69. The King is Exposed
□ #

1. e4 Nf6 2. Nc3 d6 3. Bc4 Nxe4 4. Bxf7+ (4. Nxe4 d5) Kxf7 5. Nxe4 e5 6. Qf3+ Kg8?

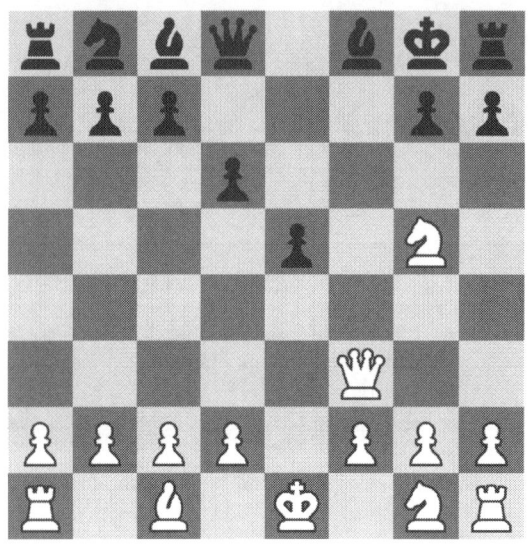

7. Ng5

Qxg5 8. Qd5+ Be6 9. Qxe6#

How to avoid the trap

After 6... Ke8 7. d4 Nc6 8. dxe5 dxe5, Black's king is displaced, but the position is still playable. The best approach is still to play 2... d5, and after 3. e5 Nfd7 4. Nxd5 Nxe5, the position is perfectly equal.

70. The O'Sullivan Gambit

■ ♗

1. e4 Nf6 2. e5 Nd5 3. d4 b5 4. Bxb5 c5 5. dxc5

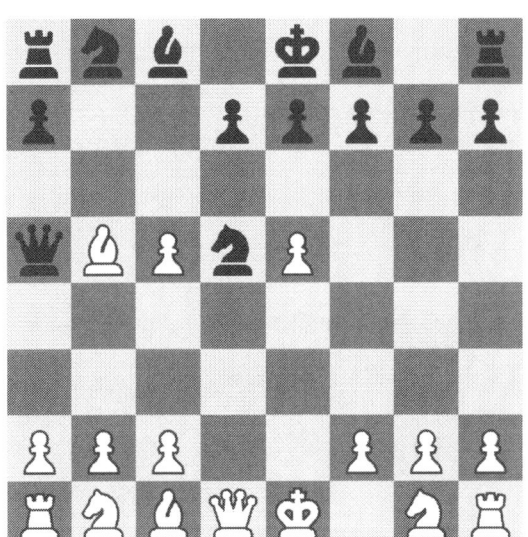

5... Qa5+

6. Nc3 Nxc3 7. bxc3 Qxb5

How to avoid the trap

After 5. Ne2 Qa5+, White can play 6. Nc3, as the knight is defended twice and White has the advantage.

Nimzowitsch Defense

The Nimzowitsch Defense begins with the moves 1. e4 Nc6

71. Knight Collapse

1. e4 Nc6 2. Nf3 d6 3. d4 Nf6 4. c3 Nxe4?

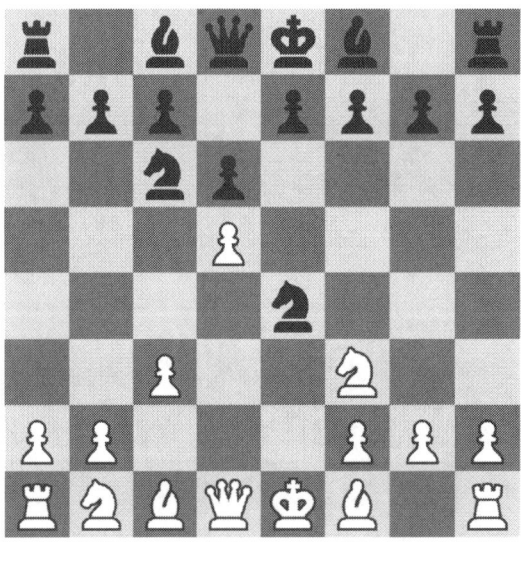

5. d5

The e4-knight is lost, for example:

- 5... Ne5 6. Nxe5 dxe5 7. Qa4+ Qxe4

- 5... Nb8 (Na5) 6. Qa4+ c6 7. Qxe4

How to avoid the trap

Black must continue their development, such as with 4... g6 5. Bd3 Bg7 6. O-O e5, resulting in balanced chances.

Gunderam Defense

The Gunderam Defense begins with the moves 1. e4 e5 2. Nf3 Qe7

72. The Fragile Knight

■ ♘

1. e4 e5 2. Nf3 Qe7 3. Bc4 Nf6 4. Ng5 h6 5. Nxf7 Rh7 6. d4 exd4 7. Qxd4

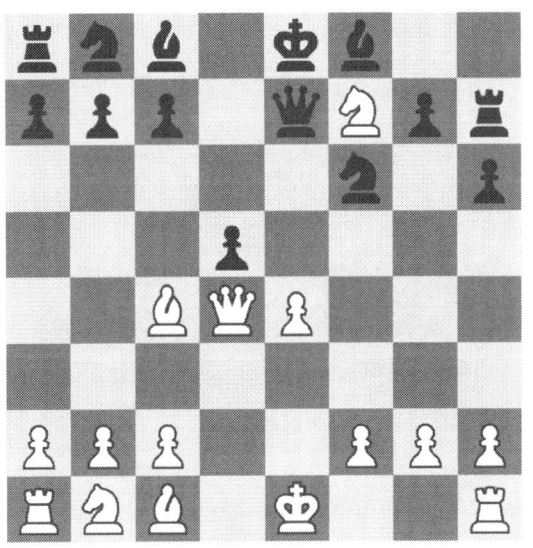

7... d5!

After 5. Bxf7 Rd8, White loses a piece.

How to avoid the trap

Objectively, the move 2... Qe7 is not a good choice, but it can be tricky. After 4. O-O, White will be able to play d4! and take control of the center. Note that after 4. O-O Nxe4? 5. Re1!, White has a crushing advantage due to the poor alignment of Black's queen and king.

1. e4 – Other Openings

73. Busch-Gass Gambit
□ ♛

1. e4 e5 2. Nf3 Bc5 3. Nxe5 Bxf2+ 4. Kxf2 Qh4+ 5. g3 Qxe4

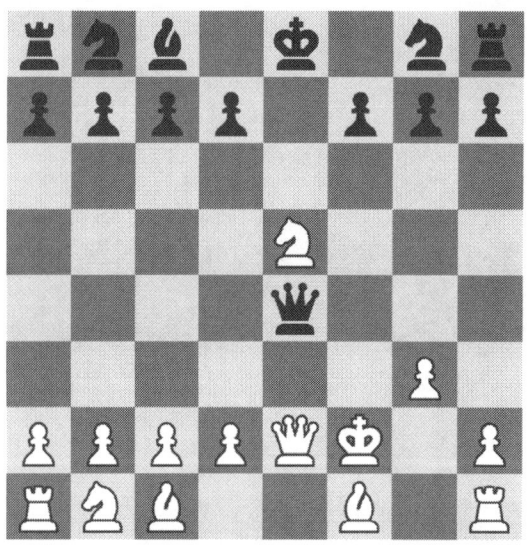

6. Qe2

Qxh1 7. Bg2 Qxc1 8. Nd3+

How to avoid the trap

2... Bc5, which offers the e5 pawn, is simply not a good move because no continuation provides Black with compensation against accurate play by White.

74. The Premature Attack

■ - +

1. e4 e5 2. Qh5 a common move among beginners Nc6 3. Bc4 g6 4. Qf3 f5 5. exf5

5... Nd4

6. Qd5 ? Qe7 7. fxg6 hxg6 8. Na3 Nf6 9. Qa5 b6 10. Qc3 Bb7 11. Nf3 O-O-O and Black has a crushing position, for example:

12. O-O Nxf3+ 13. gxf3 Qh7

How to avoid the trap

It's best not to bring out the queen too early, but the decisive mistake is 6. Qd5. Playing 6. Qg3 could still save the game because after 6... Nxc2+ 7. Kd1, taking on a1 is impossible due to 7... Nxa1 8. Qxe5+ Qe7 9. Qxh8

The Queen's Gambit

The Queen's Gambit begins with the moves 1.d4 d5 2.c4

75. The Rubinstein Trap
□ ♙/♛

1. d4 d5 2. c4 e6 3. Nf3 Nf6 4. Bg5 Nbd7 5. e3 Be7 6. Nc3 O-O 7. Rc1 Re8 8. Qc2 a6 9. cxd5 exd5 10. Bd3 c6 11. O-O Ne4 12. Bf4 f5?

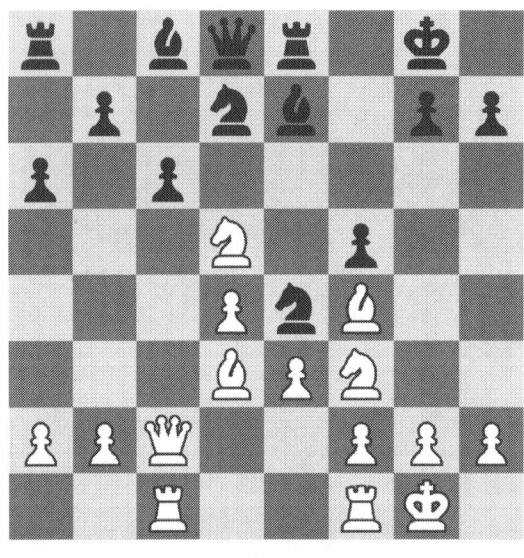

13. Nxd5!

13... cxd5?? 14. Bc7

How to avoid the trap

After 11... Ne4, White can simply capture a pawn with 12. Bxe4 dxe4 13. Nxe4. Playing 11... g6, which closes the diagonal of the d3 bishop, is stronger. The fatal mistake is 12... f5, which tries to overprotect the Ne4. After 12. Bf4, Black should have played 12... Ndf6, which equalizes.

76. A White Classic

□ ♙/♞/♗

1. d4 d5 2. c4 dxc4 3. e3 b5 4. a4 c6 5. axb5 cxb5

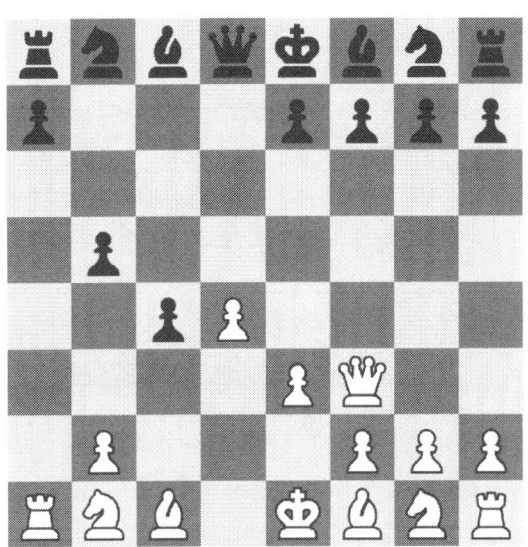

6. Qf3

How to avoid the trap

Black must return the pawn with 3... Nf6 and continue their development. If they insist on playing 3... b5, the best approach is to push the b-pawn after 4. a4 to hinder White's development. Note that after 4... a6, both 5. axb5 and 5. Qf3 are strong. If Black tries to protect the b5 pawn with the bishop, 4... Bd7 (or Ba6), then 5. axb5 Bxb5 6. Nc3 will leave Black with serious difficulties protecting both the bishop and the c4 pawn.

77. A Black Classic
■ ♘

1. d4 d5 **2.** c4 e6 **3.** Nc3 Nf6 **4.** Bg5 Nbd7 **5.** cxd5 exd5 **6.** Nxd5

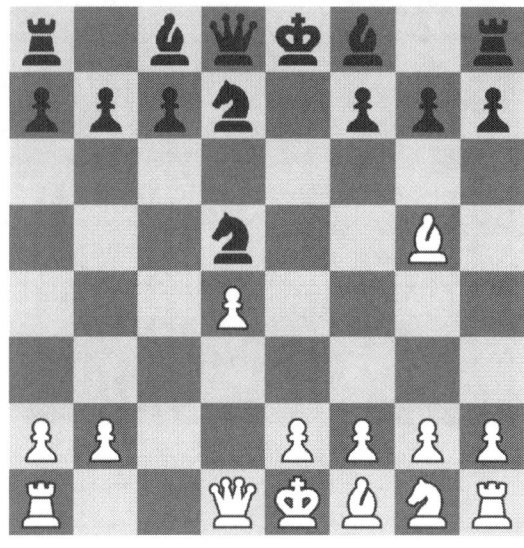

6... Nxd5

7. Bxd8 Bb4+ **8.** Qd2 Kxd8 **9.** Qxb4 Nxb4

How to avoid the trap

This trap is also known as the "Elephant Trap."
6. e3, and now the d5 pawn is threatened because the White king has an escape square.

78. Counterattack in the Center

■ ♛

1. d4 d5 2. c4 e5 3. dxe5 d4 4. e3 Bb4+ 5. Bd2 dxe3 6. Bxb4

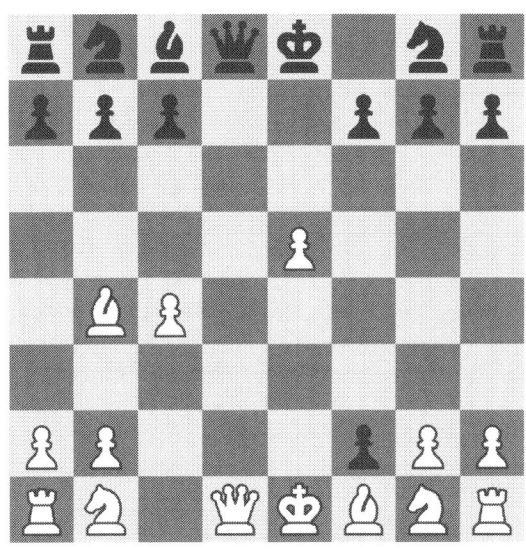

6... exf2+

7. Ke2 fxg1=N+ 8. Rxg1 Bg4+

How to avoid the trap

Even though 4. Nf3 is better for White, the decisive mistake happens on the 6th move. After 6. fxe3 Qh4+ 7. g3 Qe4 8. Nf3, the position is equal.

The Slav Defense

The Slav Defense begins with the moves 1. d4 d5 2. c4 c6.

79. A False Pin
□ #

1. d4 d5 2. c4 c6 3. Nf3 Nf6 4. Nc3 dxc4 5. e3 b5 6. a4 b4 7. Na2 a5 8. Bxc4 Bg4

9. Ne5 Bh5 10. Qxh5 Nxh5 11. Bxf7#

How to avoid the trap

The pin 8… Bg4 is a mistake because it doesn't pin anything. Black must cover f7 with 8… e6, after which they can castle and look for counterplay on the queenside.

The Nimzo-Indian Defense

The Nimzo-Indian Defense begins with the moves 1.d4 Cf6 2.c4 e6 3.Cc3 Fb4

80. One Step Too Far
□

1. d4 Nf6 2. c4 e6 3. Nf3 b6 4. Nc3 Bb4 5. Qc2 Bb7 6. Bg5 h6 7. Bh4 d6?

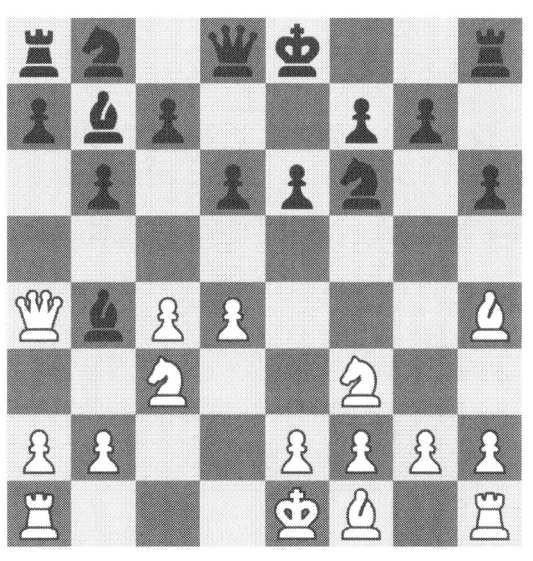

8. Qa4+

Nc6 (to defend Bb4) 9. d5

How to avoid the trap

Black must exchange their Bb4 before moving the d7 pawn, either immediately or after 7... g5 Bg3 8. Ne4 to trade off the white dark-squared bishop.

The King's Indian Defense

The King's Indian Defense begins with the moves 1.d4 Cf6 2.c4 g6 3.Cc3 Fg7

81. The Ng4 Trap in the Saemisch

1. d4 Nf6 2. c4 g6 3. Nc3 Bg7 4. e4 d6 5. f3 O-O 6. Be3 Nc6 7. Bd3 e5 8. Nge2 Ng4 9. Bd2 (9. fxg4 exd4 10. Nxd4 Nxd4)

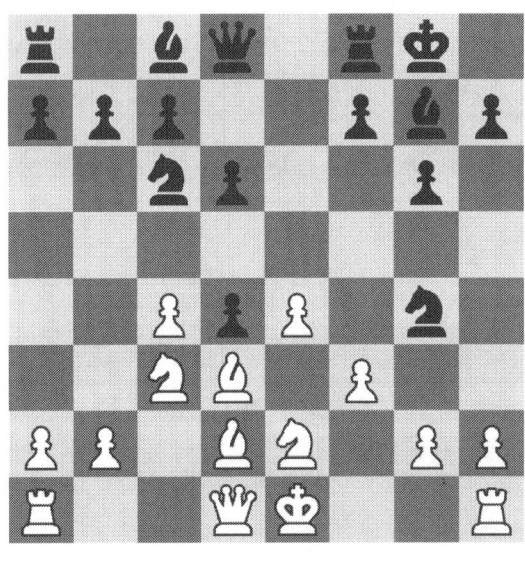

9... exd4

10. Nd5 Nge5 11. Qc2 Nxd3+ 12. Qxd3 Ne5

How to avoid the trap

By playing 9. Bd2 to protect their bishop, White ends up in a difficult position. The best response to the 7... e5 push is to play d5, closing the center and completing development.

The Queen's Indian Defense

The Queen's Indian Defense begins with the moves 1.d4 Cf6 2.c4 e6 3.Cf3 b6

82. A Beautiful Diagonal

1. d4 Nf6 2. c4 e6 3. Nf3 b6 4. g3 Ba6 5. b3 c5 6. d5

6... Nxd5

7. cxd5 Qf6 8. Qc2 Qxa1 9. Nc3? c4 10. Bg2 Bb4 and the Nc3 will fall.

How to avoid the trap

After 9. Bb2 Qxa2 10. Nc3 Qa5, White has the advantage despite the material deficit. They are better developed and will be able to attack Black's position quickly after castling.

The Benoni Defense

The Benoni Defense begins with the moves 1.d4 c5

83. A Mirrored Trap
■ ♖/♘

1. d4 c5 2. dxc5 e6 3. b4 a5 4. c3 axb4 5. cxb4

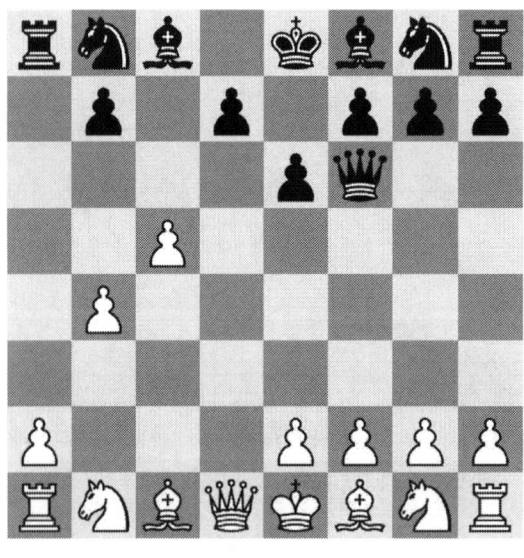

5... Qf6

and the only way to save the a1-rook is to give up the knight: 6. Nc3 Qxc3+ 7. Bd2

How to avoid the trap

This trap mirrors one encountered in the Queen's Gambit Accepted. The best way to counter the Benoni is to push the pawn: 2. d5

Other Indian Defenses

84. The Alekhine-Marshall Trap
■ #

1. d4 Nf6 2. c4 e6 3. Nf3 Ne4 4. Nfd2 Bb4 5. a3 Qf6 6. f3??

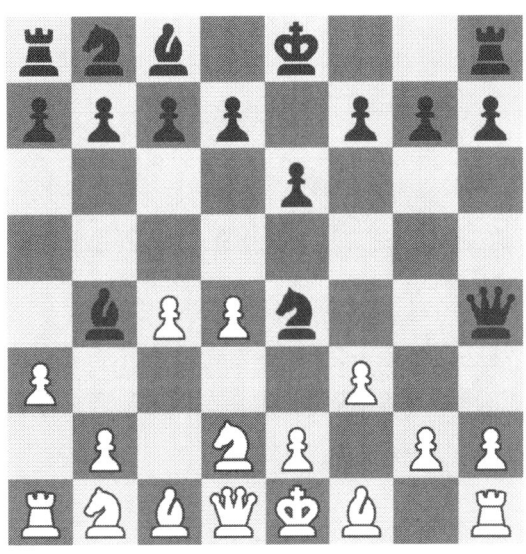

6... Qh4+

7. g3 Nxg3 8. Rg1 Ne4+
9. Rg3 Nxg3

How to avoid the trap

5. e3 is preferable to a3 because the white queen will be able to defend the f2 pawn on 5... Qf6. However, 6. f3 is a big mistake that loses immediately. White should have played 6. Qc2 to free the d1-square for the white king, even though Black's position remains better.

The London System

The London System begins with the moves d4, Bf4, and Nf3, although the move order can vary.

85. The Trapped Queen

1. d4 Nf6 2. Bf4 g6 3. e3 Bg7 4. Nf3 d6 5. Nbd2 O-O 6. h3 Nbd7 7. Bc4 Re8

8. Bxf7+

Kxf7 9. Ng5+ Kg8 10. Ne6

How to avoid the trap

7... c5 gives Black's queen some breathing room and allows them to focus their attack plan on the queenside.

86. The Poor Bishop

■ ♗

1. d4 d5 2. Bf4 h5 3. e3

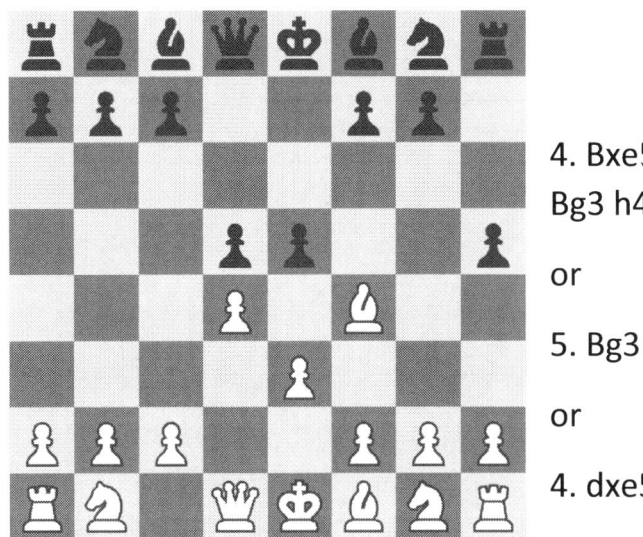

3... e5

4. Bxe5 f6 5. Bf4 g5 6. Bg3 h4

or

5. Bg3 h4 6. Bf4 g5

or

4. dxe5 g5 5. Bg3 h4

How to avoid the trap

After 2... h5, White must be cautious and play 3. Nf3 first, for example: 3... d6 4. e3, and 4... e5 no longer works because of 5. dxe5, with the g5-square being protected twice.

The Jobava Attack

The Jobava Attack is a variation of the London System beginning with the moves d4, Nc3, and Bf4.

87. Eyes on c7!

□ ♟♟♟

1. d4 d5 2. Nc3 Nf6 3. Bf4 Nc6 4. Nb5 e5 5. Bxe5 Nxe5 6. dxe5 Ne4

7. Qxd5

7... Qxd5 8. Nxc7+ Kd8 9. Nxd5

How to avoid the trap : 3... Nc6 is already a mistake due to the threat on c7, as Na6 is no longer possible to defend. Although several moves are possible, the best is still to permanently prevent Nb5 with 3... a6 or 3... c6. With precise play, Black has no trouble maintaining equality.

The Stonewall Attack

The Stonewall Attack is characterized by the moves 1.d4, 2.e3, 3.f4, and 4.c3, usually followed by 5.Bd3, though not necessarily in this order.

88. Pawn Wave

□ + -

1. d4 d5 2. e3 Nf6 3. Bd3 e6 4. Nd2 Bd6 5. f4 O-O 6. Ngf3 c5 7. c3 Nc6 8. O-O b6 9. Ne5 Bb7 10. g4 Nd7 11. g5 f6?

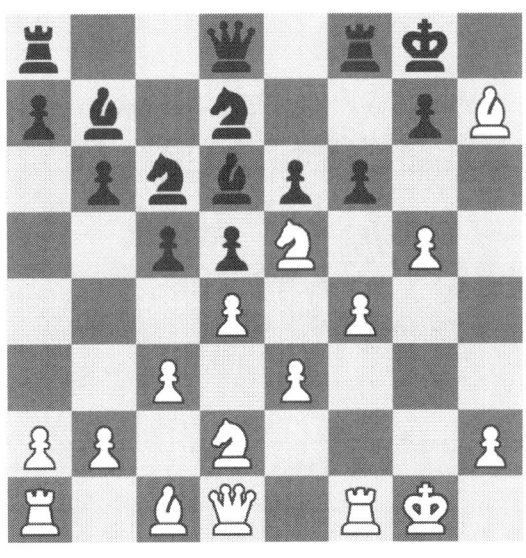

12. Bxh7+

Kxh7 13. Qh5+ Kg8 14. g6

How to avoid the trap : After 11. g5? (premature), Black must eliminate the Ne5: 11... Ncxe5 12. dxe5 Nxe5! 13. fxe5 Qxg5+ 14. Kh1 Qxe5. Black has regained material equality (a minor piece is worth three pawns) and, more importantly, has wrecked the protection around White's king, gaining a clear advantage.

The Torre Attack

The Torre Attack arises after the moves d4, Nf3, and Bg5.

89. Queen on the Horizontal
□ #/♗

1. d4 Nf6 2. Bg5 e6 3. Nf3 d5 4. e3 Be7 5. Bd3 O-O 6. Nbd2 Nbd7 7. c3 b6 8. Qa4 Bb7 9. Ne5 Nxe5 10. dxe5 Nd7

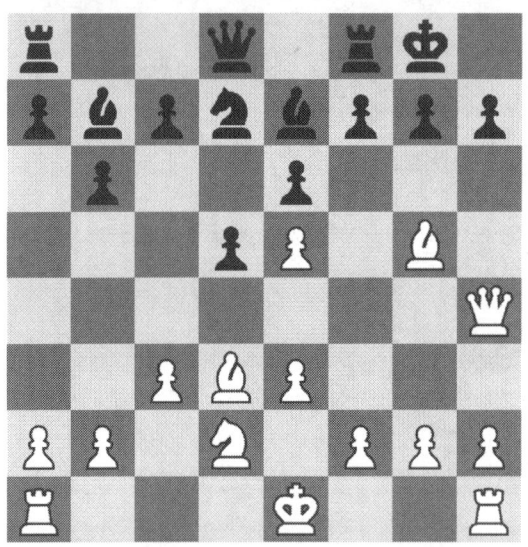

11. Qh4

Black must defend against the threat of 12. Qxh7#, and the e7 bishop is lost.

How to avoid the trap

9... c5 is better for Black than exchanging knights on e5, but it is not yet a mistake. However, retreating the Nf6 to d7 is. The move 10... Ne4 is necessary, and after 11. Bxe7 Qxe7 12. Nxe4 dxe4 13. Bxe4 Qh4! White must play 14. g4 to save the pinned bishop on e4. After 14... Bxe4 15. Qxe4, Black is a pawn up, but White has not castled, and their pawn structure is weaker.

The Albin Counter-Gambit

The Albin Counter-Gambit begins with the moves 1. d4 d5 2. c4 e5

90. Lasker's Trap
■ - +

1. d4 d5 2. c4 e5 3. dxe5 d4 4. e3? Bb4+ 5. Bd2

5... dxe3!

6. Bxb4?? exf2+ 7. Ke2 (7. Kxf2?? Qxd1) 7... fxg1=N+ 8. Ke1 (8. Rxg1 Bg4+) 8... Qh4+ 9. Kd2 (9. g3 Qe4+) 9... Nc6 10. Bc3 Bg4 11. Be2 O-O-O+

How to avoid the trap

4. Nf3, which develops a piece, is much better than 4.e3, but the real mistake is 6. Bxb4. White should have played 6. fxe3, and despite a chaotic pawn structure, Black's attack fizzles out, leaving an equal position.

The Budapest Gambit

The Budapest Gambit begins with the moves 1. d4 Cf6 2. c4 e5

91. The Fajarowicz Trap

■ ♕

1. d4 Nf6 2. c4 e5 3. dxe5 Ne4 4. Nf3 d6 5. exd6 Bxd6 6. g3??

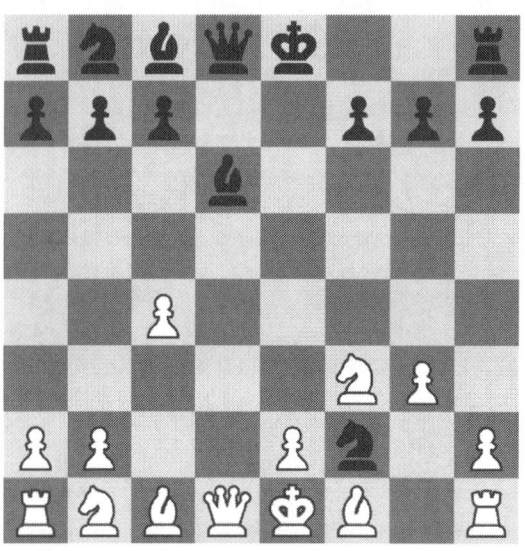

6... Nxf2!

7. Kxf2 Bxg3+

How to avoid the trap

After 3... Ne4, White should prevent the check on b4. The simple 4. a3 leaves White with an advantage since the Ne4, an easy target in enemy territory, will lose time retreating to safety. Playing 4... d6 still allowed for Qc2, giving White a clear advantage. However, the mistake is 6. g3, which allows Black's combination. White should have played 6. Nbd2, and Black's trap would have fallen apart.

The Blackmar-Diemer Gambit

The Blackmar-Diemer Gambit begins with the moves 1. d4 d5 2. e4 dxe4 3. Nc3 Nf6 4. f3

92. The Halosar Trap
□ #

1. d4 d5 2. e4 dxe4 3. Nc3 Nf6 4. f3 exf3 5. Qxf3 Qxd4 6. Be3 Qb4 7. O-O-O Bg4

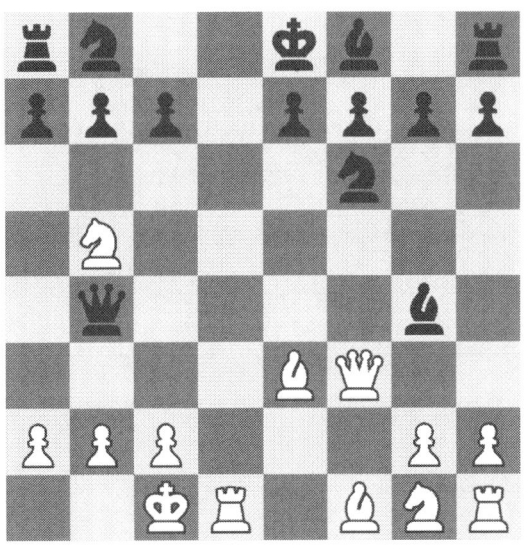

8. Nb5

Na6 9. Qxb7 Rb8 10. Qxb8+ Nxb8 11. Nxc7#

How to avoid the trap

Black must protect the b7 pawn and cover the b5-square with 7... c6 before bringing out their bishop.

The Dutch Defense

The Dutch Defense begins with the moves 1. d4 f5

93. The X Factor
☐ B-

1. d4 f5 2. g4 fxg4 3. h3 d5 4. hxg4 Bxg4 5. Qd3 Qd7 6. Rxh7 Bf5 (too greedy!)

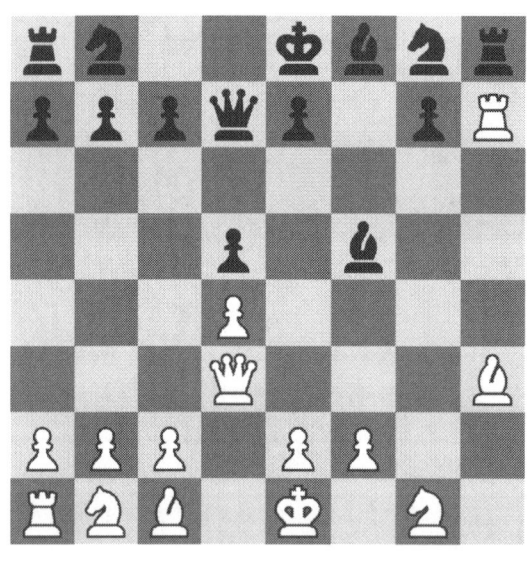

7. Bh3

Bxh3 8. Qg6+ Kd8 9. Rxh8 Be6 10. Qh7

How to avoid the trap

Black must simply exchange the rooks on h7. Their king will be displaced after 6. Rxh7 Rxh7 7. Qxh7 Nf6 8. Qg6+ Kd8, but after 9. Nc3 Nc6 10. Bf4 Nxd4 11. O-O-O c5, the position is equal.

94. A Miniature
□ #

1. d4 f5 2. e4 fxe4 3. Qh5+ g6 4. Be2? gxh5??

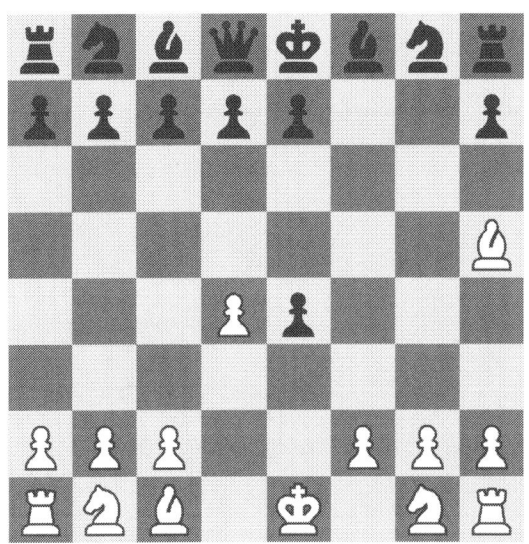

5. Bxh5#

How to avoid the trap

4. Be2 sets a trap but is weak because after 4... Nc6 5. d5 e6 (or Nf6), the white queen must retreat, leaving White with a development problem.

The Englund Gambit

The Englund Gambit begins with the moves 1. d4 e5

95. The Englund Gambit Trap
■ #

1. d4 e5 ?! 2. dxe5 Nc6 3. Nf3 Qe7 4. Bf4 Qb4+ 5. Bd2 Qxb2 6. Bc3?

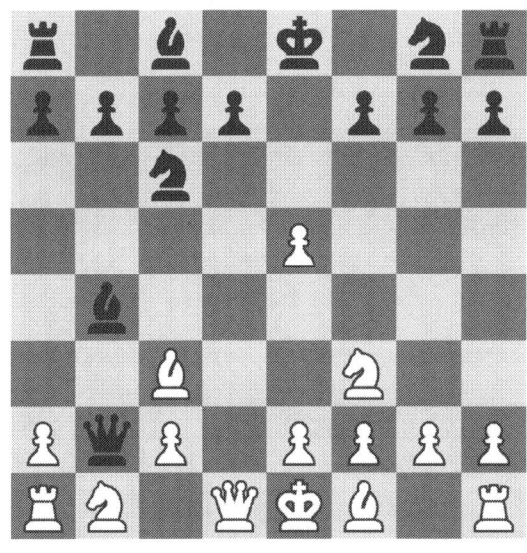

6... Bb4

7. Qd2 Bxc3 8. Qxc3 Qc1#

How to avoid the trap

After 5... Qxb2, White must continue development with 6. Nc3!, and after 6... Bb4 7. Rb1 Qa3 8. Rb3 Qa5 9. e4, White will soon be able to castle and eliminate their difficulties.

96. A Queen or Nothing

1. d4 e5 2. dxe5 Bc5 3. Nf3 d6 4. exd6 Ne7 5. dxe7

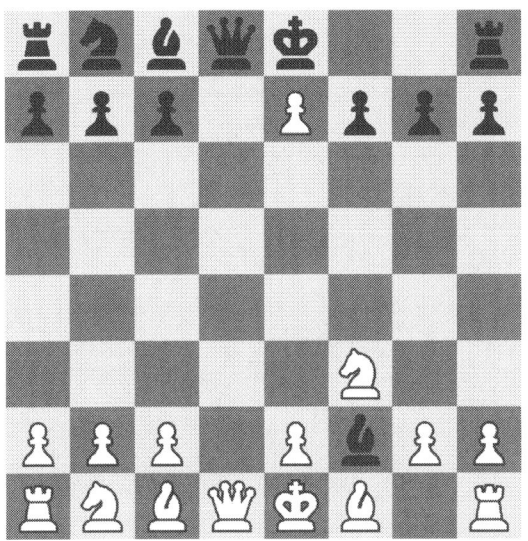

5... Bxf2+

6. Kxf2 Qxd1

How to avoid the trap

Blitz players often "pre-move" 4... Ne7 to make it appear like a blunder. However, 5. e3, which blocks the a7-g1 diagonal, and 5. Nc3, which defends d1, are much better moves and leave White with a strong advantage.

97. Again, a Queen or Nothing
■ ♛

1. d4 e5 2. dxe5 d6 3. exd6 Bxd6 4. Nf3 Nc6 5. Nc3 Bg4 6. e3 Qe7 7. Be2 O-O-O 8. O-O Bxf3

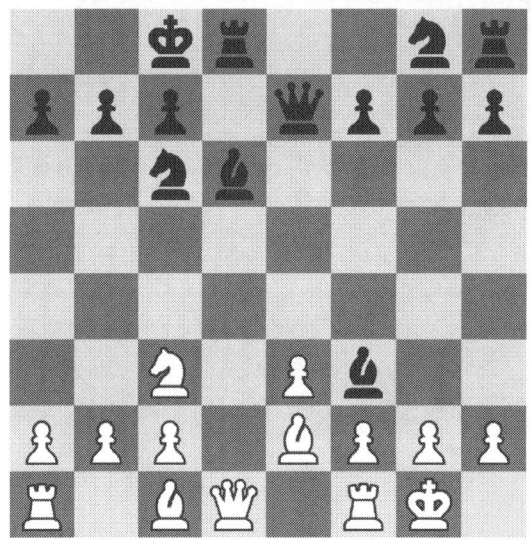

9. Bxf3

Bxh2+ 10. Kxh2 Rxd1

How to avoid the trap

White should have covered the d-file with 8. Bd2 or Nd4, retaining a slight advantage.

The English Opening

The English Opening begins with the move 1. c4

98. English Trap for Beginners

1. c4 d5 2. cxd5 Nf6 3. e4 Nxe4

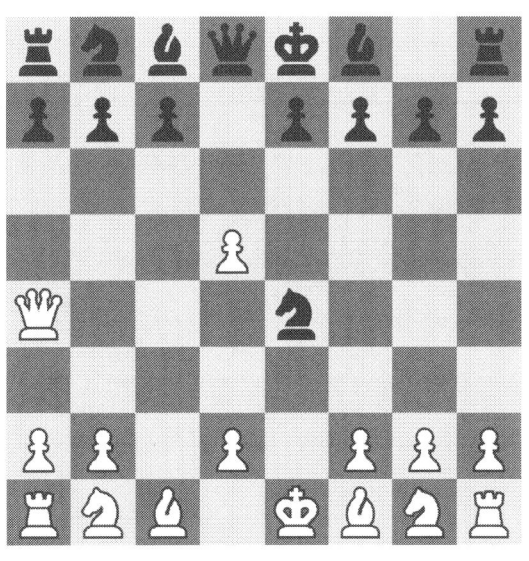

4. Qa4+

How to avoid the trap

The mistake is 3... Nxe4. Black's first two moves are not the most common but are playable if one wants to attempt the Schulz Gambit with 3... c6.

99. The Untouchable Queen
■ #

1. d4 Nf6 2. c4 c5 3. Nf3 cxd4 4. Nxd4 e5 5. Nb5 d5 6. cxd5 Bc5 7. d6 Ne4 8. Nc7+

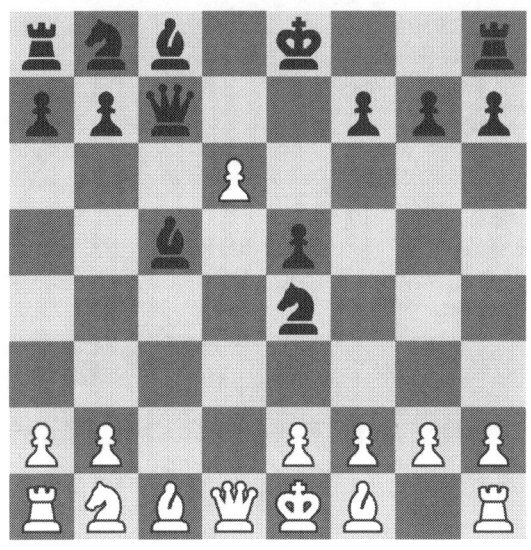

8... Qxc7

9. dxc7 Bxf2#

How to avoid the trap

White must absolutely maintain control of e4 to deny access to the Nf6 (always dangerous with the bishop on c5), either by retreating the Nb5 to c3 or by playing 7. e3

Other Openings

100. A Strange Checkmate
□ #

1. Nc3 g6 2. d3 Bg7 3. Qd2 e6 4. Ne4 Ne7 5. Qh6 Bxh6

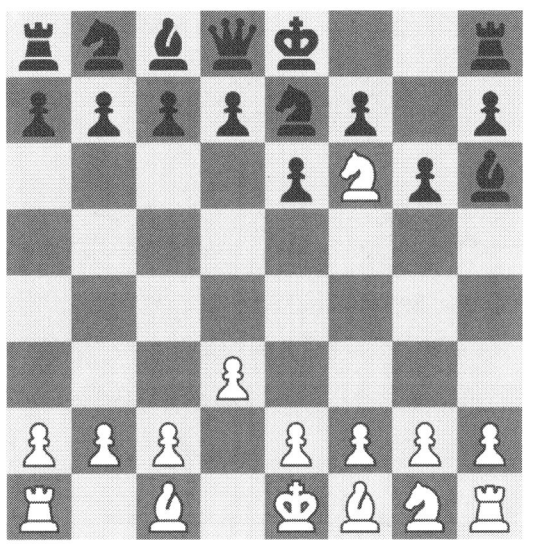

6. Nf6+

Kf8 7. Bxh6#

How to avoid the trap

This miniature occasionally appears online in bullet games. Even though the queen looks tempting, Black must castle here: 5... O-O 6. Qh4 f6, and White's attack is over, leaving Black with the advantage.

Acknowledgments

First and foremost, I would like to express my heartfelt gratitude to everyone who has supported me throughout the creation of this book. To my family and friends, thank you for your patience, encouragement, and belief in me.

To my teachers, mentors, and sparring partners at the chessboard, thank you for sharing your wisdom and pushing me to continuously improve, not just as a player but also as a creator.

A special thanks to my readers—you are the reason this book exists. Your passion for chess inspires me, and I hope that this work contributes to your growth and enjoyment of the game.

Lastly, I extend my thanks to the global chess community, a remarkable group of thinkers and competitors who remind me every day why this ancient game continues to thrive.

Bob

Share Your Thoughts

If you've enjoyed this book or found it helpful in your chess journey, I would be grateful if you could take a moment to leave a review online. Your feedback not only helps others discover this book but also inspires me to continue creating content for chess enthusiasts like you.

Thank you—and may your chess games be full of brilliant moves and lifelong lessons!

Printed in Great Britain
by Amazon

6d76cdcf-c27e-4247-87c0-a9dd8ecd266fR01